TWENTIETH CENTURY INTERPRETATIONS
OF

VANITY FAIR

A Collection of Critical Essays

Edited by

M. G. SUNDELL

Prentice-Hall, Inc. A SPECTRUM BOOK   *Englewood Cliffs, N. J.*

Current printing (last number):

10   9   8   7   6   5   4   3   2

PRENTICE-HALL INTERNATIONAL, INC. (*London*)
PRENTICE-HALL OF AUSTRALIA, PTY. LTD. (*Sydney*)
PRENTICE-HALL OF CANADA, LTD. (*Toronto*)
PRENTICE-HALL OF INDIA PRIVATE LIMITED (*New Delhi*)
PRENTICE-HALL OF JAPAN, INC. (*Tokyo*)

Contents

Introduction, *by M. G. Sundell*   1

PART ONE—*Interpretations*

Vanity Fair, by Arnold Kettle   13

On *Vanity Fair, by Dorothy Van Ghent*   27

Vanity Fair, by Kathleen Tillotson   40

On the Style of *Vanity Fair, by G. Armour Craig*   55

Vanity Fair: An Irony Against Heroes, *by A. E. Dyson*   73

Form, Style, and Content in *Vanity Fair, by John Loofbourow*   91

PART TWO—*View Points*

Frank W. Chandler: Becky as a Rogue   107

Percy Lubbock: Thackeray's Authorial Intrusion   109

E. M. Forster: Becky as a "Round Character"   110

Edwin Muir: The Novel of Character   111

Geoffrey Tillotson: "Panorama" and "Scene"   111

Walter Allen: Thackeray's Trivial View of Life   113

Joseph E. Baker: Thackeray and St. Augustine   114

E. M. W. Tillyard: Vanity Fair: A Picaresque Romance   115

Table of Serial Publication of Vanity Fair   *118*

Chronology of Important Dates   *119*

Notes on the Editor and Contributors   *121*

Selected Bibliography   *123*

Acknowledgments

Unfortunate omissions are inevitable in books of this kind. I regret especially that I have lacked space to tell more about Thackeray's life and to include comments on *Vanity Fair* by Mr. Gordon Ray, the most notable student of Thackeray. The length of Mr. Ray's pertinent essays and their resistance to excerption prevented me from reprinting them. I am grateful for the help and advice of Mr. Arthur Adrian, Mr. Roger Salomon, Mrs. Esther Scheps, Mr. Frederik Smith, Mrs. Nina Sundell, and especially Mrs. Anne Wyatt-Brown. I owe thanks to Dean Lester Crocker of Case Western Reserve University for providing funds for the preparation of my manuscript.

Introduction

by M. G. Sundell

Thackeray's best work, *Vanity Fair,* was also his first important novel and the making of him critically and financially. Its success transformed him within a few months from one among the horde of skilled London literary men known only in the trade into a recognized major writer. By January of 1848, while the book was still in serial publication, Thackeray could justly gloat to his mother that, after a decade of struggling to establish himself, he had suddenly "become a sort of great man in [his] way—all but at the top of the tree: indeed there if the truth were known and having a great fight up there with Dickens." [1] For the rest of his life Thackeray was able to command large sums and serious attention as a novelist, essayist, editor, and public lecturer in Britain and the United States.

Before the first monthly number of *Vanity Fair* appeared in January, 1847, Thackeray had tried his luck with other extended works of fiction, among them *Catherine* in 1839–40 and *Barry Lyndon* in 1844, but he had published them under pseudonyms and with no great success. For income, he had depended mainly on a standard mixture of Grub-Street jobs: reviews of literature and painting, parodies, Christmas books, travel sketches, humorous pieces of various sorts. He had even served a term as political correspondent in Paris for the *Constitutional.* Some of the works of these years are delightful, notably *The Snobs of England,* published in 1846 and early 1847, which set Thackeray up as the leading contributor to *Punch.* None, however, has anything like the substance of the great novels, nor could the profits from such labor, even augmented by those from the illustrations Thackeray often drew for his books and articles, permit him to live as a gentleman, while assuring the future support of two small daugh-

---

[1] *The Letters and Private Papers of William Makepeace Thackeray,* ed. Gordon N. Ray, 4 vols. (Cambridge, Mass., 1945–46), II, 333.

ters and an incurably insane wife. By 1847, he had considerable need of the triumph with which *Vanity Fair* provided him.

The circumstances of Thackeray's birth and youth do not foreshadow his later worries about money and social rank. The family of his father, Richmond Thackeray, was one among the many that, during the eighteenth century, attained full respectability in England while joining in the plunder of India, easily accomplished under the lax rule of the East India Company. William Thackeray was born on January 11, 1811, in Calcutta, where he spent his first five years before being sent home to England, according to Anglo-Indian custom, for education. His mother followed in 1820, now the wife of Captain Henry Carmichael-Smyth, a girlhood sweetheart she had married in 1817, two years after her first husband's death. Meanwhile, William grew up in the same fashion as other upper-middle class Englishmen of the time, differing from the ordinary most noticeably in his dislike of sports. After attending small preparatory schools, he entered Charterhouse early in 1822. There he received the usual bad public-school education but had the luck to fall in with boys who stimulated his interest in literature and art. In February, 1829, he matriculated at Trinity College, Cambridge. In his year and a half at the University, he made a close friend of Edward FitzGerald, read a good deal of modern literature, and wrote for an undergraduate periodical prophetically called *The Snob,* but chiefly he cultivated his taste for good-living, partly by trips to Paris, at least one of them surreptitious. Rounding off his liberal education with six months in Weimar to learn German, he met Goethe—a "bright, clear, and rosy" old man of eighty speaking French "with not a good accent" (*Letters,* III, 444)—and gained the recollections later to inform the Pumpernickel chapters of *Vanity Fair.* Then, in May of 1831, Thackeray settled in London, ostensibly to study law but actually to live as a wealthy young man-about-town.

The bulk of both Thackeray's and the Carmichael-Smyths' fortunes was involved in the great Indian commercial houses, many of which failed in the early 1830s. By December, 1833, having lost most of his patrimony in the general collapse, Thackeray needed to prepare himself seriously to earn a living. No longer able to face the prospect of the law, he at first tried to develop his talent for drawing by studying painting in London and then in Paris, but he soon perceived accurately that he had little real ability. Economic necessity became sharper in August, 1836, when he married Isabella Shawe, a pleasant but weak Irish girl, apparently rather like David Copperfield's "child-wife" Dora and probably one of the models for Amelia Sedley.[2] In the following March, Thackeray moved from Paris to London in search of free-lance work as a writer. The decade of literary journeymanship which ensued was marked by a good deal of Bohemian living, the birth of three daughters (one of whom died in infancy), moments of real financial trouble, and the mental deterioration of Isabella Thackeray, leading to her permanent removal from her family in 1845.

Although biographers who find moral and intellectual good fortune in worldly affliction are often insufferably complacent, such a conclusion seems justified in the case of Thackeray. Certainly he considered himself lucky to have been forced to work hard, and certainly, too, his tastes inclined him to be a dilettante and voluptuary. From the long training in periodical writing necessitated by poverty, Thackeray gained much professionally: he developed a beautifully supple style; he learned to meet a deadline, even during his frequent attacks of great physical pain from stricture of the urethra; he became intimate with the artistic and social *demi-monde* which provided some of his best subjects.

Besides compelling him to master his trade, Thackeray's difficulties surely demanded the sharp thought about the importance of money, conduct, and social rank which informs what Gordon Ray calls the leading theme of his mature works: the redefinition of "the gentlemanly ideal to fit a middle-class rather than an aristocratic context."[3] The evidence of *Vanity Fair*—particularly illustrated by the younger Osbornes, Sedleys, and Dobbins—shows the close bond in Thackeray's day between wealth and respectability. Moreover, though a gentleman might properly write as a hobby and a great man like Dickens gain acceptance anywhere, a hack writer—even a superior one—of the sort Thackeray was for ten years was automatically suspect socially. By becoming a professional literary man, Thackeray inevitably weakened his social position, already made fragile by his loss of fortune. Proud of his heritage and upbringing as a gentleman, he could not have avoided analyzing the nature of gentility in order to justify and

[2] The others seem to have been his mother and Jane Brookfield, the wife of a Cambridge friend and Thackeray's great love. For the most extensive discussion of Thackeray's use of real people as models for his characters, see Gordon N. Ray's *The Buried Life: A Study of the Relation between Thackeray's Fiction and His Personal History* (London, 1952).

[3] Gordon N. Ray, *Thackeray*, 2 vols. (New York, 1955–58), I, 13. I have drawn heavily on this book for the biographical information in this Introduction.

maintain this pride. Nor could he have escaped remorse for his blindness to Isabella's unhappiness during the early years of their marriage. The result of such thought appears in *Vanity Fair* most clearly in the contrast between George Osborne, the parody of a conventional hero, and the awkward William Dobbin. Osborne, who behaves worst when aping his social betters, treats his wife and all the world as if they existed only to admire his adornment of the social position to which he pretends and aspires. Dobbin, a fool in his love of Amelia and affection for George, nonetheless sets a standard of true gentility in his diligence, benevolence, and delicate consideration of others. Though not always so obvious, this concern to divorce gentility from questions of rank, wealth, and flashy manners pervades the novel, showing in such disparate ways as the ironic growth of Rawdon Crawley from aristocratic buck to middle-class gentleman under the influence of Becky Sharp, the elevation to dignity of the ridiculous Mrs. O'Dowd and the more ridiculous Miss Swartz by their kindness to Amelia, and the indictment of accepted standards of virtue implicit in Becky's accurate reflection: "I think I could be a good woman if I had five thousand a year" (XLI, 409).[4]

Accompanying this criticism of current mores is an attack, sharp though rarely explicit, on the organizations which embody the values of society. Thackeray makes them seem at best inefficient, at worst corrupt. Personifying institutions by the men who serve them, he sets up a satiric portrait gallery of fools and knaves, whose very presence in public life constitutes a condemnation of the established order. Thus, he shows Parliament mainly in the persons of Lord Steyne and the two Sir Pitt Crawleys, whose names imply their moral natures, as do those of many other inhabitants of Vanity Fair. The established Church appears as the High and Dry Bute Crawley, amiable and dense, who hunts or sleeps off his wine while his wife composes his sermons. Less appealing, if anything, are the Dissenters, represented by the overbearing Lady Southdown—an aristocratic Mrs. Pardiggle—and her tract-writing daughter. General Tufto, a padded flirt, personifies the upper echelons of the army, for Thackeray makes clear that the competent and brave Michael O'Dowd reaches command only through unusual good luck. Embodying the colonial and foreign services are Joseph Sedley, Rawdon Crawley, the younger

---

[4] I quote *Vanity Fair* from Geoffrey and Kathleen Tillotson's authoritative Riverside edition, giving chapter as well as page numbers. The Introduction to this edition is an excellent critical and textual essay.

Pitt Crawley—formerly *attaché* at Pumpernickel—and Tapeworm, *chargé d'affaires* there, who carries on mock-epic warfare with his French counterpart. In a deliciously ironic reminiscence inspired by Becky's presentation to George IV, Thackeray satirizes even the Crown, in the person of "the First Gentleman of Europe":

> Do you remember, dear M———, oh friend of my youth, how one blissful night five-and-twenty years since, the Hypocrite being acted, Elliston being manager, Dowton and Liston performers, two boys had leave from their loyal masters to go out from Slaughter House School where they were educated, and to appear on Drury Lane stage, amongst a crowd which assembled there to greet the king. THE KING? There he was. Beef-eaters were before the august box: the Marquis of Steyne (Lord of the Powder Closet,) and other great officers of state were behind the chair on which he sate, *He* sate— florid of face, portly of person, covered with orders, and in a rich curling head of hair—How we sang God save him! . . . Yes, we saw him. Fate cannot deprive us of *that.* Others have seen Napoleon. Some few still exist who have beheld Frederick the Great, Doctor Johnson, Marie Antoinette, &c.—be it our reasonable boast to our children, that we saw George the Good, the Magnificent, the Great. (XLVIII, 459)

No more a social and political theorist than Dickens, Thackeray does not offer a better alternative to the organization of society he portrays so sharply. Indeed, any such theory would be irrelevant to his artistic vision, since he views, as does Dickens, particular social evils as manifestations of general moral evil. For this reason, despite Thackeray's great care about historical detail, *Vanity Fair* does not essentially describe only the second and third decades of the nineteenth century. Changing fashions, for example, demand that Bute Crawley's son Jim be a more somber clergyman than his father, and Thackeray records this change; but he makes clear that the change is merely one of appearances. Jim has no more vocation than Bute, and the Church will remain a trumpery as long as men confuse their religious professions with belief. Similarly, even should the unacknowledged warfare pictured in the novel between the upper and middle classes be resolved, society will be no healthier until people value wealth, comfort, and prestige less than kindness, diligence, honor, and love. Thackeray's portrait of a world socially and economically corrupt provides supporting evidence for socialist arguments, but it is drawn by a moralist, not an economist—more in the spirit of Carlyle than of Marx.

The view of human nature animating *Vanity Fair* is bleak.

Though some of the characters are attractive and even endearing, almost all are egoists, motivated by a desire for the comfort of physical ease and high prestige or for the more subtle comfort of self-esteem. Often, of course, it is difficult to distinguish between vices wholly social in origin and those rooted in inherent human weakness, but the faults of the major characters cannot in any instance be traced fully to the organization of society. Thus, although old Sir Pitt's querulousness may result partly from the inhibitions of rank that kept him from following his natural bent as a lawyer, his rage at learning that he has been bested in the courtship of Becky by his son—not by some stranger—can have no such cause. Rather, it clearly derives from innate parental envy equally apparent in his consequent frantic affair with Betsy Horrocks of the Ribbons, a lesser Miss Sharp. Moreover, the Baronet's behavior informs us that we are to read as other manifestations of the paternal jealousy of grown sons Mr. Osborne's intense anger at George's marriage and his absurd proposal to the rich mulatto he had picked for the boy, Lord Steyne's triumph at his heir's sterile marriage and his second son's insanity, and perhaps even Mr. Sedley's merciless teasing of a Jos rendered bashful by the presence of the youthful Rebecca.[5]

One might cite innumerable other examples of selfishness, usually wedded to self-delusion, as subtly drawn as those showing a father's efforts to retain his self-esteem by defeating or controlling his son. A few must suffice. Miss Crawley assumes the virtue of sentimental feelings and democratic views wholly belied by her actions. George Osborne, immediately after his honeymoon, thinks himself a model husband for establishing his lonely wife in a splendid hotel suite while he goes off for a night with the boys. Later, Amelia spoils her child, ignores her parents' troubles, and tortures Dobbin in conceiving of herself as a romantic heroine—a widow of supreme fidelity to a husband she wilfully distorts in remembrance into a knight and lover beyond reproach. Almost everyone in the book shows this mixture of egoism and self-deception. The major exceptions are Dobbin and Becky, each of whom escapes one of these faults while being caught by the other. Dobbin, considerate of everyone he meets, ruins much of his own life by his perverse refusal to view Amelia and his relation to her accurately. Becky, unremittingly selfish, is at least blessed with a refreshing clarity about her own motives, behavior, and attrac-

---

[5] Dorothy Van Ghent discusses this motif extensively in the essay reprinted in this volume (see pp. 27–39 below).

tions. Together, they demonstrate the impossibility of anyone's avoiding fully the Fair of Vanities. The character of the other personages in the novel is well illustrated by this anecdote which Thackeray offers as an exemplum of both essential human nature and the particular social vices it inspired at the moment of which he writes:

> It was but this present morning, as he rode on the omnibus from Richmond; while it changed horses, this present chronicler, being on the roof, marked three little children playing in a puddle below, very dirty and friendly and happy. To these three presently came another little one. *"Polly,"* says she, *"your sister's got a penny."* At which the children got up from the puddle instantly, and ran off to pay their court to Peggy. And as the omnibus drove off I saw Peggy with the infantine procession at her tail, marching with great dignity towards the stall of a neighbouring lollipop-woman. (XXIII, 217–218)

We are almost all, Thackeray says, both Peggy and her courtiers.

Moved thus by vanity or destroyed by the vanities of others, the characters of the novel together form a brutal, sterile, and fragmented world. Balancing the cluster of violent old men, furious at their sons, is a group of forlorn spinsters, clutching at husbands, lusting for other women's children, or nursing romantic interludes from the distant past. Jane Osborne yearns for Amelia's son and recalls her brief flirtation with her drawing-master, as she withers in her father's house, "working at a huge piece of worsted . . . hard by the great Iphigenia clock" (XLII, 414). Her desiccated governess, Miss Wirt, foreshadows what Jane will become, save in wealth. Miss Briggs, also cherishing the memory of a youthful affair, expends her sentiment on anyone who will tolerate it. Glorvina O'Dowd dances and shakes her ringlets fruitlessly through countless seasons on two continents. Many women who do marry are little better off. The second Lady Crawley, having sold herself for a title, sustains her husband's abuse by working perpetually at a worsted of her own, since she lacks "character enough to take to drinking" (IX, 83). Lady Steyne suffers similar abuse and mourns her sons. Amelia adopts the unwilling spinsters' sentimentality and sterility during her best years in her idolatry of the dead and worthless George. Almost all the families which survive jealousy become fragmented through avarice or social pride. The Crawleys compete in preying upon rich Miss Crawley, and Briggs' relatives mimic them by seeking the modest fortune of Miss Crawley's companion.

Mrs. Frederick Bullock, *née* Maria Osborne, ignores her father and sister as unworthy of her new social eminence. In the background of this terrible portrait of the world are insanity and violence. Madness, which runs in the noble blood of the Steynes, also threatens Amelia after Waterloo and fitly marks the end of Sir Pitt. Lord Steyne dies in the clutches of a second-rate courtesan. Jos Sedley, having spent his great lusts on curries and waistcoats and having escaped his valet's razor, is at best worried to death by Becky. George dies in the bloodbath of patriotism, the scene more stark for being underplayed, and the remarks with which Thackeray prefaces the account of his death picture war as a prettified tribal version of the immoral brutality congenital to man:

> You and I, who were children when the great battle was won and lost, are never tired of hearing and recounting the history of that famous action. Its remembrance rankles still in the bosoms of millions of the countrymen of those brave men who lost the day. They pant for an opportunity of revenging that humiliation; and if a contest, ending in a victory on their part, should ensue, elating them in their turn, and leaving its cursed legacy of hatred and rage behind to us, there is no end to the so-called glory and shame, and to the alternations of successful and unsuccessful murder, in which two high-spirited nations might engage. Centuries hence, we Frenchmen and Englishmen might be boasting and killing each other still, carrying out bravely the Devil's code of honour. (XXXII, 314)

Despite the harshness of this picture, *Vanity Fair* amazingly remains a comic novel, rarely approaching even what we now call "black humor." Those who read it as a Dostoevskyan rendering of hell-on-earth distort it even more than those who make it a proto-Marxist tract. The tone with which Thackeray tells the story, though occasionally bitter, is more often genial and accepting. Many of the characters and situations are simply funny. The scene of Lady Bareacres stuck in her coach in Brussels awaiting horses may suggest the immobility of the aristocracy and the general stagnation of England, but it is primarily amusing. So are countless others. Even some of the characters who most strongly convey an oppressive sense of sterility or brutality also contribute to the humor. The amorous spinster and the interfering father, for example, are stock comic figures almost as old as Western literature, and Thackeray sometimes portrays his Jane Osbornes and Sir Pitts as such traditional buffoons, ridiculous for the discrepancy between their desires and fact. He does not, of course, treat them only in this way. Miss Osborne and Sir Pitt are individuals as well as types. Jane is as capable of suffering as of silliness. The Baronet, dangerous as no father in Plautus or his imitators truly is, can also feel real anguish. A sign of Thackeray's artistry is his ability to make his characters at once conventional butts and distinct people who compel our joy, fear, or sympathy because of the particularity of their pleasure, rage, or pain. This achievement is part of what seems to me his central triumph in the novel: making us accept even the worst in his terrible world as inevitable, sad, funny, and valuable because it is human.

The major device by which Thackeray gains this effect is the character he assumes as storyteller of the novel. More subtly than Emily Brontë in *Wuthering Heights* or Dickens in *Bleak House*— the other two masterpieces of fiction published near mid-century —Thackeray makes his narrative method the apt vehicle of his artistic vision. This method depends on our accepting as both real and authoritative the fictitious Thackeray who addresses us. Witty and avuncular, well-travelled, well-dined, and well-read, capable of both sentimentality and moral precision, the narrator possesses a richness of personality, variety of experience, and sharpness of intellect which demand respect. Yet he is himself an inhabitant of Vanity Fair, like the people of whom he speaks—and, he insists, like the rest of us too. He overvalues a good dinner; he has toadied to a lord; he can become infatuated with his characters, finding Amelia and Becky charming while admitting their silliness and vice. He even takes a childish pleasure in teasing his audience —withholding information, forcing us to acknowledge our own vanities, insisting at one moment that his story is fiction, at the next that it is fact. Indeed, Thackeray presents the very composition of the novel as the narrator's chief vanity, as a grand frivolity —a grand game of one-upmanship on his part. The fictitious story-teller thus becomes to an extent a personification of Vanity Fair, mitigating by his attractiveness the bitter flavor of the world he portrays and embodies. More importantly, his wisdom induces our concurrence in his essential response to that world and compels us to agree that, since human behavior is immutable and man's life short, we should laugh at particular follies while rebuking them, accept particular vices while condemning them. He persuades us further that we should cherish the transient vitality of even the wicked as unique, however closely each individual may resemble all others past and to come.

The presence of the narrator, a consistent dramatic creation despite his human inconsistencies, unifies *Vanity Fair* by causing us to perceive its sprawling world through the filter of a single consciousness. One need only glance at *Henry Esmond,* far different in idiom, to recognize the careful tailoring of the style of each novel to the personality and situation of its ostensible author. Thackeray further unifies *Vanity Fair* by its moral congruity, which I have already noted, and by multiple comparisons and contrasts of the characters' natures and adventures. Chief among these, of course, are the correspondences between Becky and Amelia, who constantly illuminate each other, though they meet only occasionally. Becky is unfeeling and usually clear-eyed; Amelia sentimental and usually deluded. Becky is active and tenacious; Amelia passive but equally tenacious. Both are selfish—the one intentionally, the other unconsciously. Repeatedly, they show their contrasting modes of tenacity and selfishness—in their treatment of their sons, their responses to poverty, their reactions to their husbands' departure for battle. The plots they inhabit correspond in many small ways. By their marriages both deprive their lovers of anticipated wealth. Both triumph on joining the army. Both give birth at almost the same moment. From near the beginning of the novel, as the fortunes of one rise, those of the other fall. Though Thackeray does not draw this contrast with an engineer's precision, he makes it sufficiently clear to provide the narrative backbone of the work, emphasizing it especially at two crucial encounters between the characters on the continent. Becky, on the make socially from the moment she leaves Miss Pinkerton's, triumphs in Brussels at the time of Waterloo and maintains her success for almost a decade. Amelia, on the make romantically, suffers a catastrophe at the great battle and passes the ensuing years isolated in widowhood and poverty. When the women meet again in Pumpernickel, their fortunes have been reversed. Becky has lost her social position through her betrayal of Rawdon, and Amelia has gained a new romance—of which she is still unaware—through the return of Dobbin. At the end of the novel, their circumstances stand in roughly the same relation as they did at the beginning. Both are well-enough off, with Amelia probably the better satisfied of the two, since William's indifference cannot be as distressing to her as pious respectability must be boring to the self-proclaimed Lady Crawley.

Employing this method generally, Thackeray enhances the unity of the novel by making all his characters foils for various other members of the Fair. Miss Briggs, for example, while casting light on her fellow spinsters and on the group of rich relatives ripe for bilking, also illuminates the other sentimentalists in the book. Silly but sincere, she acts as a light parody of Amelia and as a contrast to the hypocritical Miss Crawley. By her unchanging susceptibility, she accentuates the growth of Lady Jane from a similar tender female into a woman of quiet firmness. In addition, her true if misguided affection for Miss Crawley emphasizes the unfeeling selfishness of Miss Crawley's relations, and her motherliness to young Rawdon points up Becky's egoism at its worst. Taking color from these other characters while coloring them in return, Briggs thus fits into several paradigms of human behavior and embodies several of the patterns which provide the thematic structure of *Vanity Fair*.

Although Thackeray succeeds by such devices in making his novel artistically coherent, he does not form it with the jeweler's nicety of a Jane Austen or a Henry James, and any attempt to describe it as a well-wrought urn is likely to prove more ingenious than exact. In part, the narrative looseness of the book may reflect Thackeray's partiality for the familiar essay, a genre marked by the fluidity of conversation. Probably a greater influence on the organization of *Vanity Fair* was the serial mode of publication. Forced to produce a set number of words every month, Thackeray inevitably padded on occasion. Moreover, in addition to insuring the overall coherence of the work, he had to plan the structure of each installment, create in each sufficient suspense to hold interest for a month, and gauge from his audience's responses what developments might increase the novel's sales.

Detailed study of any monthly part suggests Thackeray's care about such matters. In the fifth, for example, he concentrates on the marriages of his major female characters, clarifying the mystery of Becky's and presenting the reconciliation of Amelia and George, separated earlier in the installment by the family quarrel resulting from Mr. Sedley's bankruptcy. By the end of the number, both girls have overcome their romantic troubles, but both now face threats of poverty and physical danger as the young couples prepare for war, disowned by their wealthy relations. While focusing on the two romances and the reactions they engender, Thackeray also compares various sentimentalists—Dobbin, Miss Briggs, and Miss Crawley—and suggests the transience of human relationships by darkening the new unions he portrays with accounts of the dissolution of old ties of family and friendship. In the course of the installment, he has moved his story along slowly, answering some questions and raising others. Meanwhile, to attract additional readers and refresh the memories of old ones, Thackeray has presented a fair sampling of the book as a whole, telling of both sets of major characters, emphasizing important themes, and maintaining the personality of the narrator in commentaries and asides.

The progression of this kind of novel must be leisurely, and its form loose. Even Dickens' middle and later works, though more elaborately constructed than *Vanity Fair,* sometimes proceed heavily and discursively. Any absolute objection to these traits, the results of the conditions of novel-writing when the novel was becoming the major literary form, seems to me critically prissy, a silliness akin to blanket attacks on the popular qualities in Shakespeare's plays. Managed well, as Thackeray manages them in *Vanity Fair,* the necessities of Victorian serial fiction permit general—though not lapidary—coherence. Furthermore, they provide an author time, as he unwinds the strands of his story, to develop a relationship of progressive intimacy like that we experience in real life between his audience and the characters and narrator of his book. This feeling must have been extraordinarily intense for Thackeray's first readers, forced to savor the novel for a year and a half, alert to topical allusions meaningless to us, and no doubt specially pleased to read in a winter installment of Christmas at Queen's Crawley or in a summer one of bathing and promenading at Brighton. Even robbed of these effects, *Vanity Fair* retains an amplitude and intimacy which, together with the exactitude of its picture of life, make it great.

PART ONE

Interpretations

Vanity Fair

by Arnold Kettle

Thackeray's method in *Vanity Fair* is in all essentials the method of Fielding in *Tom Jones*. To call the method panoramic, as many critics do (and in particular Mr. Percy Lubbock in *The Craft of Fiction*) is true but can be misleading. It is true in the sense that Thackeray's vision shifts about, that he surveys a broad field of territory and that the reader is kept at a certain distance from the scene.

The core of *Vanity Fair* is not a developing emotional situation involving the intense experience of a limited number of characters. We do not get "inside" one particular character and see the action through the imprint upon his consciousness, nor do we become so closely involved in a concrete situation (seeing it, so to speak, backward and forward and from many angles) that we have a sense of encompassing the whole complex of forces that makes such a situation vital. Even at a big dramatic moment, such as the famous scene when Rawdon Crawley returns from the spunging-house and finds Becky and Lord Steyne together, we do not have the effect of a vital clash of conflicting forces.

We wonder what is going to happen, we relish the theatrical quality of the scene; but our emotions are not deeply engaged because we know that nothing truly disturbing or exquisitely comic will be revealed; nothing will be changed, neither Becky nor Rawdon nor Steyne nor us. Even the ambiguity which Thackeray is at pains to achieve—"was Becky innocent?"—does not succeed in making us look at the scene in a fresh way, because the issue is

"Vanity Fair." *From* An Introduction to the English Novel *by Arnold Kettle (London: Hutchinson & Co. [Publishers] Ltd., 1951; New York: Harper & Row, Publishers, 1960), pp. 156–70. Copyright held by Arnold Kettle. Reprinted by permission of Hutchinson & Co. [Publishers] Ltd. The numbering of footnotes has been slightly altered for the sake of clarity.*

morally a false one. Whether Becky is actually Steyne's mistress or
not scarcely matters. And Thackeray knows it scarcely matters; with
the result that the raising of the issue gives the impression of a
sexual archness rather than that of a genuine ambiguity, the effect
of which would be, by raising an important doubt in our mind, to
make us suddenly see the episode in a new way, with a new flash
of insight.

Everything in *Vanity Fair* remains at a distance because between
the scene and the reader there always stands, with an insistent
solidity, Thackeray himself. Of course it is true that every novelist
stands between the scene of his novel and the reader, controlling
and directing our attention. But by a Jane Austen or an Emily
Brontë or a Dickens the directing is done, not necessarily un-
obtrusively (we are always aware of Dickens especially), but with
an eye primarily on the object or the scene that is being revealed,
whereas with Thackeray one has constantly the sense that the scene
itself is less important than something else.

Take, for example, the very first episode of *Vanity Fair*, the
great scene of the departure of Amelia and Becky from Miss
Pinkerton's academy in Chiswick Mall, at the climax of which
Becky throws the dictionary out of the coach window into the
garden. It is a beautifully and dramatically conceived scene, an
episode that is to tell us more about Becky than fifty pages of
reminiscence; but notice how Thackeray handles the climax:

> Sambo of the bandy legs slammed the carriage-door on his weep-
> ing mistress. He sprang up behind the carriage. "Stop!" cried Miss
> Jemima, rushing to the gate with a parcel.
>
> "It's some sandwiches, my dear," said she to Amelia. "You may be
> hungry, you know; and Becky, Becky Sharp, here's a book for you that
> my sister—that is, I—Johnson's Dictionary, you know; you mustn't
> leave us without that. Good-bye. Drive on, coachman. God bless
> you!"
>
> And the kind creature retreated into the garden, overcome with
> emotions.
>
> But, lo! and just as the coach drove off, Miss Sharp put her
> pale face out of the window, and actually flung the book back into
> the garden.
>
> This almost caused Jemima to faint with terror.
>
> "Well, I never," said she; "what an audacious—" Emotion pre-
> vented her from completing either sentence. The carriage rolled
> away. . . .[1]

[1] *Vanity Fair*, Chap. I.

This is excellent, but there is one word in the passage that prevents the scene from being fully dramatic and stops it achieving its potential force—the word "actually" in the sentence describing the flinging of the book. This one word colours the scene, investing it with a sense of scandalized amazement which may well reflect Miss Jemima's feelings but which weakens (not disastrously, of course, but appreciably) the objective force of the episode. After all, we know without that adverb what Miss Jemima's feelings are; its only function in the description is in fact to bring a particular colouring to the scene. It is Thackeray who steps in and in stepping in reduces the whole episode. The tone of that "actually" is the tone that puts almost everything in *Vanity Fair* at a distance.

Does it necessarily matter, this distancing of a novel by its author? I do not think it matters at all if it is a successful part of a consistent plan. Fielding achieves it very successfully in *Tom Jones,* so does Samuel Butler in the greater part of *The Way of All Flesh.* But the method, it must be recognized, puts an enormous strain on the author. If we are to be constantly seeing a novel through a kind of haze of reflectiveness spread around it by the author, then the comments, the reflections, the qualities of mind of the writer have got to be distinguished by quite remarkable understanding and control. We have seen how, in *Oliver Twist,* the conscious attitudes of Dickens are very frequently inadequate to what he is portraying. With Dickens this does not matter very much because his dramatic method concentrates the whole attention on the developing scene and makes the comment unimportant (one can mentally skip it without doing violence to the novel).

But with Thackeray's method the opposite holds. Everything depends on the capacity of the novelist to encompass in his own personality an adequate attitude to what he is describing. If he succeeds he will indeed cast around his puppets that understanding and humanity which (in Henry James's words about Fielding) do "somehow really enlarge, make everyone and everything important." But if his attitudes are less than adequate, then by driving his characters into the distance he will be weakening his whole effect.

The description "panoramic" may become misleading when applied to *Vanity Fair* if the word suggests that the individual characters in Thackeray's novel are not important, that the book has anything of the nature of the documentary. Mr. Lubbock (whose pages on Thackeray are consistently stimulating) seems to me on rather dangerous ground when he writes:

Not in any single complication of incident, therefore, nor in any single strife of will, is the subject of Vanity Fair to be discerned. It is nowhere but in the impression of a world, a society, a time— certain manners of life within a few square miles of London, a hundred years ago. Thackeray flings together a crowd of the people he knows so well, and it matters not at all if the tie that holds them to each other is of the slightest; it may easily chance that his good young girl and his young adventuress set out together on their journey, their paths may even cross from time to time later on. The light link is enough for the unity of his tale, for that unity does not depend on an intricately woven intrigue. It depends in truth upon one fact only, the fact that all his throng of men and women are strongly, picturesquely typical of the world from which they are taken, that all in their different ways can add to the force of its effect. The book is not the story of any one of them, it is the story that they unite to tell, a chapter in the notorious career of well-to-do London.[2]

There is so much that is true here that it may seem a little pedantic and ungenerous to insist that it is not altogether helpful. It is indeed true that the subject of *Vanity Fair* is a society—the world of well-to-do Britain (not merely London) at the beginning of the last century. But it is also true that this subject is seen in terms not of a general impression but of specific human relationships. "An impression of manners" is not an accurate description. As we look back on Thackeray's novel we recall a whole world, a bustling, lively, crowded world; but we recall it in terms of individual people and their relationships. These people are presented to us, by and large, in the tradition of the comedy of humours. That is to say each has particular characteristics, somewhat exaggerated and simplified, by which they are easily comprehensible.

"These characters are almost always static," Mr. Edwin Muir has said.

They are like a familiar landscape, which now and then surprises us when a particular effect of light or shadow alters it, or we see it from a new prospect. Amelia Sedley, George Osborne, Becky Sharp, Rawdon Crawley—these do not change as Eustacia Vye and Catherine Earnshaw do; the alteration they undergo is less a temporal one than an unfolding in a continuously widening present. Their weaknesses, their vanities, their foibles, they possess from the beginning and never lose to the end; and what actually does change is not these, but our knowledge of them.[3]

[2] *The Craft of Fiction* (1921), p. 95.
[3] *The Structure of the Novel* (1946 ed.), p. 24.

This is, broadly speaking, true, but not quite fair. Some of the characters in *Vanity Fair* do change; Pitt Crawley, for instance, who begins as a simple unworldly prig, blossoms out with a fortune into an ambitious worldly idiot, and yet remains the same person, and particularly Amelia who, in her infuriating way, develops a good deal in the course of the novel.[4] The important point, however, is that Thackeray's puppets (it is a pity he used the word, for it has encouraged an underestimation of his subtlety) are all involved in human relationships which, though not presented with much intimacy or delicacy of analysis, are for the most part true and convincing relationships.

We know, for instance, quite precisely enough the quality of George Osborne's feeling for Amelia or of Rawdon's for Becky. The latter relationship could scarcely be better illustrated than by the letter Rawdon writes from the spunging-house:

"Dear Becky" (Rawdon wrote),—"*I hope you slept well.* Don't be *frightened* if I don't bring you in your *coffy*. Last night as I was coming home smoking, I met with an *accadent.* I was *nabbed* by Moss of Cursitor Street—from whose *gilt and splendid parler* I write this—the same that had me this time two years. Miss Moss brought in my tea—she is grown very *fat*, and as usual, had *her stockens down at heal*.

"It's Nathan's business—a hundred and fifty—with costs, hundred and seventy. Please send me my desk and some *cloths*—I'm in pumps and a white tye (something like Miss M's stockings)—I've seventy in it. And as soon as you get this, Drive to Nathan's—offer him seventy-five down, and ask *him to renew*—say I'll take wine— we may as well have some dinner sherry; but not *picturs*, they're too dear.

"If he won't stand it. Take my ticker and such of your things as you can *spare*, and send them to *Balls*—we must, of coarse, have the sum to-night. It won't do to let it stand over, as to-morrow's Sunday; the beds here are not very *clean*, and there may be other things out against me—I'm glad it an't Rawdon's Saturday for coming home. God bless you.

"Yours in haste,
"R. C."

"*P.S.*—Make haste and come." [5]

<hr>

[4] One or two characters change quite unconvincingly, not because they develop organically but because Thackeray seems to change his plans for them half-way through. Lady Jane Sheepshanks (who marries Pitt Crawley) is one of these. Some critics consider that Amelia changes in this way only, but I think the evidence is against them.

[5] *Vanity Fair*, Chap. LIII.

Every sentence of this is masterly. Thackeray is marvellously good at depicting typical upper-class young men—the sketch of James Crawley with his "dawgs" is a delightful minor example—the kind of people of whom Matthew Arnold wrote: "One has often wondered whether upon the whole earth there is anything so unintelligent, so unapt to perceive how the world is really going, as an ordinary young Englishman of our upper class." [6] Now it is true that we do not enter intimately into the feelings of any of these characters, but it would be wrong to suppose they are any the less human. When we say we know the quality of their feelings what we mean is that we know all *about* those feelings, not that we share them in the way we share Emma's responses. But it is not, even in the very broadest sense, their manners that are the subject of the book.

The central relationship with which Thackeray, like Fielding and Richardson and Jane Austen, is concerned is marriage. *Vanity Fair* is about the difficulties of personal relationships, particularly marriage relationships, in nineteenth-century, upper-class English society. It is a well-organized novel despite its discursiveness and some lapses in construction (the most clumsy being the return to England of Dobbin and Joseph Sedley; the chronology and therefore what has been well called the choreography is very confused here). The planning of the double story of Becky and Amelia is by no means as casual as Mr. Lubbock would seem to suggest. Not only do the two girls stand in a complementary relation to each other—the one active and "bad," the other passive and "good"—but their careers are juxtaposed in contrasting curves of development, Becky's curve rising in the centre of the book, Amelia's declining. The fact that from the death of George at Waterloo to the reunion at Pumpernickel the two women scarcely meet does not weaken the pattern of the book nor blur the underlying contrast between them, for each is playing her necessary part.

Lord David Cecil in his essay on Thackeray notices the strong pattern of the book but seems curiously imperceptive as to its significance.

> The characters of the two girls are designed to illustrate the laws controlling Vanity Fair as forcibly as possible. And in order to reveal how universally these laws work, they are of strongly-contrasted types.
>
> Amelia is an amiable character, simple, modest and unselfish. But,

[6] *Culture and Anarchy* (1932 ed.), p. 84.

says Thackeray, in Vanity Fair such virtue always involves as a corollary a certain weakness. Amelia is foolish, feeble and self-deceived. She spends a large part of her youth in a devotion, genuine enough to begin with, later merely a sentimental indulgence in her emotions, to a man unworthy of her. For him she rejects a true lover; and though she is ultimately persuaded to marry this lover, it is only, ironically enough, through the chance caprice of the woman for whom her first love had rejected her. Nor is she wholly saved from the punishment of her error. By the time he marries her, her true lover has learnt to see her as she is.

Becky, the second "heroine" is not weak and self-deceived; she is a "bad" character, a wolf not a lamb, artful, bold and unscrupulous. But she, no more than Amelia, can escape the laws governing the city of her nativity. By nature a Bohemian, she is beguiled, by the false glitter surrounding the conventional rank and fashion which are the vulgar and predominant idols of Vanity Fair, to spend time and energy in trying to attain them. She succeeds, but she is not satisfied. Nor is she able to maintain her success. She is too selfish to treat the husband, who is necessary to her position, with the minimum of consideration necessary to keep him. She sinks to the underworld of society. But her eyes are not opened; and the rest of her life is spent in trying to retrieve herself, so far successfully that we see her last as a charitable dowager, a pattern of respectability, a final flamboyant example of the deceptiveness of outward appearances in Vanity Fair.

This parallel structure extends to the men who enter Amelia's and Becky's lives; they are similarly contrasted, similarly self-deceived. . . .[7]

This appears to me a remarkable example of criticism gone wrong, missing the essential point of the novel under consideration. To write of Becky as "beguiled by the false glitter surrounding the conventional rank and fashion, etc." is surely to miss the vital question: what else could Becky do? And once we ask that question it becomes irrelevant to talk of self-deception. Lord David Cecil, having insisted that the book is about a society, Vanity Fair, then proceeds to abstract the characters morally from that society and discuss them as though they had any existence outside it. Because he sees the individual and society as separate entities and social "laws" as something abstract and distinct from personal moral standards he misses the vital motive-force of the novel.

The trouble with Becky is not that "she is too selfish, etc." (It is not selfishness of that type that leads to the intrigue with Lord

Steyne, nor is the keeping of a husband in that sense Becky's greatest necessity.) Becky's dilemma—and Amelia's for that matter —is the dilemma of Jane Fairfax in *Emma* and of almost all the heroines of English fiction from Moll Flanders onwards. What is a young woman of spirit and intelligence to do in the polite but barbarous world of bourgeois society? Only two courses are open to her, the passive one of acquiescence to subjugation or the active one of independent rebellion.[8] The only hope of a compromise solution is the lucky chance of finding an understanding man like Mr. Darcy or Mr. Knightley, rich enough to buy certain civilized values and kind enough to desire them; but the snag is that the Mr. Knightleys require something Becky by her very fate (she has had a harder fight than Jane Fairfax) can never have—"true elegance of mind." You cannot pick that up in Soho or slaving for Miss Pinkerton.

Becky, like Moll and Clarissa and Sophia (each after her own fashion) before her, rebels. She will not submit to perpetual slavery and humiliation within the governess trade. And so she uses consciously and systematically all the men's weapons plus her one natural material asset, her sex, to storm the men's world. And the consequence is of course morally degrading and she is a bad woman all right. But she gains our sympathy nevertheless—not our approving admiration, but our human fellow-feeling—just as Heathcliff does, and she too gains it not in spite but because of her rebellion. She gains it from the moment she flings kind Miss Jemima's dictionary out of the window and thereby rejects the road that would have led her to become a Miss Jemima herself. It is this act that sets in motion the vital vibrations of the book, and

[8] It is interesting to notice how in *Vanity Fair* as in the eighteenth-century novels the one thing that none of the important characters (however hard pressed) ever contemplates doing is physical work. For a woman the job of governess or companion is degradation enough, below that is unthinkable, however critical one's situation, and as a last resort prostitution is a greatly preferable alternative to labour. As for men, the typical solution—credit and the generosity of relatives breaking down—is a commission in the Army. This failing, Newgate or the spunging-house is the next step, with the extreme possibility of a life of crime. But no one ever becomes a worker and the reason is obvious. Once one had passed from the owning to the labouring class one was lost. One never got back and life, to one who had once known the standards of the civilized world, was simply not worth living. George Osborne found he could not possibly live on two thousand a year; but it is left to Amelia to discover that "women are working hard, and better than she can, for twopence a day." (Chap. L.)

it is interesting to compare it with that other act of rebellion that sets off so vastly different a book as *Wuthering Heights*.

There is no mystery about the vitality and fascination of Becky Sharp. It is not a sentimental sympathy that she generates. Thackeray, the Victorian gentleman, may tone down her rebellion by ambiguous adverbs and a scandalized titter, but the energy he has put into her is more profound than his morals or his philosophy and she sweeps him along. Of course Becky is unadmirable (though for the moment when she tells Amelia the truth about George Osborne, "that selfish humbug, that low-bred cockney-dandy, that padded booby, etc.," one can forgive her much), but what else could she have been?

> "It isn't difficult to be a country gentleman's wife," Rebecca thought. "I think I could be a good woman if I had five thousand a year. I could dawdle about in the nursery, and count the apricots on the wall. I could water plants in a green-house, and pick off dead leaves from the geraniums. I could ask old women about their rheumatisms, and order half-a-crown's worth of soup for the poor. I shouldn't miss it much, out of five thousand a year. I could even drive out ten miles to dine at a neighbour's, and dress in the fashions of the year before last. I could go to church and keep awake in the great family pew; or go to sleep behind the curtains and with my veil down, if I only had practice. I could pay everybody, if I had but the money . . . !" [9]

In other words she could have been, with luck, someone not unlike Mrs. Elton in *Emma*, though she would have played her cards a good deal better. She could alternatively, of course, have had a shot at being Amelia. Amelia also could be a very good woman (by Victorian standards) on five thousand a year and at the conclusion of the book is in this happy condition. But not before the consequences of being Amelia have been pretty thoroughly shown up, even to the wooden old war-horse, Dobbin.

Amelia is often regarded as one of Thackeray's failures, the weak link in *Vanity Fair*. I think this is because too many readers want her to be something she cannot be within the pattern of the book —a heroine. Certainly as a heroine she cuts a very feeble figure. Certainly, too, there is a recurring ambiguity in Thackeray's attitude to her. If we tend to think of her as a heroine *manquée* it is largely his fault, for in the first part of the novel it is hard to

[9] *Vanity Fair*, Chap. XLI.

believe that his comments on poor, tender, abused little Amelia are in any deep sense ironical. And yet if we expect too much of Amelia we can not put all the blame on Thackeray. We are warned in the first chapter by the tone of: "She had twelve intimate and bosom friends out of the twenty-four young ladies . . ." And by Chapter XII we should realize that Amelia is not being produced for our uncritical approval:

> . . . in the course of a year (love) turned a good young girl into a good young woman—to be a good wife presently when the happy time should come. This young person (perhaps it was very imprudent in her parents to encourage her, and abet her in such idolatry and silly, romantic ideas), loved, with all her heart, the young officer in his Majesty's service with whom we have made a brief acquaintance. She thought about him the very first moment on waking; and his was the very last name mentioned in her prayers. She never had seen a man so beautiful or so clever; such a figure on horseback: such a dancer: such a hero in general. Talk of the Prince's bow! what was it to George's? She had seen Mr. Brummell, whom everybody praised so. Compare such a person as that to her George! . . . He was only good enough to be a fairy prince; and oh, what magnanimity to stoop to such a humble Cinderella! . . .[10]

(Here again Thackeray does not play quite fair. It is pretty clear that the "goods" of the first sentence are not to be taken quite at their face-value, but the tone of "silly, romantic ideas" is highly ambiguous. Against whom is the irony directed?) Certainly after fifteen years of self-deception as widow no one can go on taking Amelia as deserving our unqualified sympathy. And indeed the whole section dealing with the Sedleys' life at Fulham is done with a realism that precludes uncritical attitudes. Had Thackeray been by this time wallowing in the kind of sentimentality which many readers feel is implicit in his attitude to Amelia, he would scarcely have permitted himself the realism of allowing young George to leave his mother with barely a regret. Nor would he have risked the final description of his heroine as a "tender little parasite."

No, Amelia is no more the heroine of *Vanity Fair* than Becky. She is, rather, the opposite possibility, the image that Becky might have chosen to become. And it is Thackeray's merit that he shows us Amelia as she is, a parasite, gaining life through a submission that is not even an honest submission, exploiting her weakness, deceiving even herself.

[10] *Ibid.*, Chap. XII.

The weakness in the pattern of *Vanity Fair* lies not in Amelia (despite the ambiguities I have referred to) but in Dobbin. It is he who lets down the novel, not merely because he is in the psychological sense unconvincing, but because he fails to bear the weight of the positive values implicit in the pattern of the book, values which, had they been successfully embodied, would have made of this novel a greater *Tom Jones,* a real comic epic in prose.

Dobbin begins as a sheepish but sensitive schoolboy fighting the snobs, but as the novel proceeds he becomes a sort of clothes-horse of the respectable middle-class virtues. He is shrewd and cultured (young George Osborne finds him a mine of information during their trip through Europe) but simple and steadfast. How any man of such sense and character could remain utterly in love, in quite an adolescent way, with Amelia all those years Thackeray can neither explain nor convince us. Perhaps his is a case of arrested development in the emotional sphere? But no, there is no such suggestion to be found. We are to take Dobbin seriously. He is not a hero but he is a rock, or rather an oak, the rugged old oak around which the tender parasite clings.

The effect of Dobbin is to keep, obscurely but nevertheless quite definitely, in the background of the novel a wooden sort of norm, an average but good man, certainly not a rebel yet just as certainly untainted by the values of Vanity Fair. It is because he is thus untainted that Dobbin is psychologically unconvincing as a character and useless to the pattern of the book. For Thackeray's great strength, by and large, is his ability to see his characters as parts of a concrete social situation. His concern, for instance, with financial details in his novel is an example not of a trivial naturalism but of his power of setting his people so firmly in the world that we believe in them completely even though we know comparatively little about them.

We do not know very much, when all is said, about Becky herself. We can only guess how happy she is, what qualms she may have, precisely what emotions drive her to act as she does. We do not know how much she likes Rawdon and her unkindness to her child is not quite convincing. She is, as we have noticed, always at a distance. And yet she is emphatically there, alive beyond a doubt, one of the great characters in all fiction. How does Thackeray do it? Fundamentally, I suggest, by this precise and firm placing of a character in a concrete social situation. We may not be told very much about what Becky *feels* but we know exactly what her situation is. We know her relationship, financial and social

(in the broadest sense), with every other character in the book and
we know the guiding principle of her conduct, that she wants to
be mistress of her own life.

And so the psychological gaps, the gaps in analysis, the ambiguities surrounding her do not matter much. Indeed there is a
sense in which their absence is a positive strength, for most such
analysis in novels involves unreal abstraction, presents problems of
character in a static way and diverts attention from the reality
of the character's actions by an exclusive concentration on his
motives. In a very important sense we know more about Becky than
about, say, Proust's hero. Like Oliver Twist and Jeanie Deans
she has a typical, symbolic quality which makes her an individual
and yet more than an individual.

This sort of typicality is regarded by some critics as a weakness
in art. To say of a character that he is a type is supposed to show
a deficiency, a failure to individualize on the part of the author.
But in fact characters in literature who are in no sense typical cannot well be artistically interesting. If Hamlet were an isolated creature, a being whose individuality made him essentially and utterly
different from other individuals, a neurotic who had lost touch
with the typical contours of human existence and relationships, he
would not be a great artistic character. He is in fact no less an
individual for being a type, a fact which Shakespeare recognized
well enough when he presented him in the convention of the
melancholic man, a class of character easily recognizable by and
significant to the Elizabethan audience.

The artistic type (and here we see the value of the old theory of
"humours" despite its psychological crudity) is not an average, not
a lowest common multiple of human characteristics, but rather the
embodiment of certain forces which come together in a particular
social situation to create a peculiar kind of vital energy. Molière's
miser is not a typical man in the sense of being an average man,
but he is a type, a more-than-individual as well as a very definite,
unique individual. Charlie Chaplin on the screen is not an average
man (no one has ever seen anybody quite like him) and yet he is
unmistakably typical, not just an oddity for all his uniqueness, but
somehow more typical of the "little man," the individual worker
in our industrial society, than any little man we actually know; and
in this lies his greatness.

Thackeray's best characters seem to me types in just this sense,
and it is this quality that gives them their vitality despite their
distance from the reader, the limits to our knowledge about them

and the crippling inadequacy of Thackeray's comments. Becky is an unmistakable individual, yet she is every woman of spirit rebelling against the humiliations forced on her by certain social assumptions. Old Osborne, similarly, is every successful nineteenth-century business man, encased in a gloomy, luxurious ugliness in that big house in Russell Square. How solid he is! How all respectable England trembles at the horror of his anger when he hears his son has married a bankrupt's daughter! How a whole world and its values comes crowding up as he leans over and speaks to his grandson when he hears of old John Sedley's death:

> "You see," said old Osborne to George, "what comes of merit and industry, and judicious speculations, and that. Look at me and my banker's account. Look at your poor grandfather, Sedley, and his failure. And yet he was a better man than I was, this day twenty years—a better man, I should say, by ten thousand pound." [11]

Thackeray himself does his best to destroy his picture of the ruling-class world. Only at certain moments will he remove himself from the position of chorus and allow the scene to make its full effect. Then his talent for the extreme and the bizarre is given full scope. Old Osborne reacting to George's death; the wicked old Sir Pitt Crawley, helpless, dumb and half-insane, sobbing pitifully when left in the charge of a servant-girl; Lady Bareacres sitting in her horseless carriage in Brussels; the description of Lord Steyne's house and family: such episodes are extraordinarily successful. But constantly, throughout the whole novel, the effect produced by what the characters do is weakened or dissipated by the author's comments.

It is not so much the sense of these comments as their tone that is disastrous. It is an ambiguous tone. In the worst of senses it is vulgar. Thackeray's attitude to nearly all his main characters—and especially Amelia and Becky—is ambiguous. And the ambiguity does not arise from subtlety, a sense that the whole truth can never be told, that there is always a complicating factor in every judgment; it comes from pusilanimity, from a desire to expose illusions and yet keep them.

The artistic motive-force of *Vanity Fair* is Thackeray's vision of bourgeois society and of the personal relationships engendered by that society. That is what his novel is about. And the sweep and vividness of it, the vitality of Becky, the rich and teeming comic life of the panorama, all derive from the insight and honesty of

[11] *Ibid.,* Chap. LXI.

Thackeray's vision. He pierces the hypocrisies of Vanity Fair, reveals the disgusting, brutal, degrading sordidness behind and below its elegant glitter. It is the heyday of bourgeois society that he paints, the days when an expanding economy could for a while carry along the hangers-on through the credit it generated (this is how Becky and Rawdon manage to live well on nothing a year) despite its pitiless rejection of its failures like old John Sedley. And the human feeling of Thackeray rebels at this society. And yet . . . and yet . . . doesn't he rather like it? To put the doubt in literary terms: is *Vanity Fair* a novel of utter integrity, as *Wuthering Heights* is?

The human indignation is constantly diluted by the clubman's bogus mellowness, not the mellowness of Fielding which is based on the real (though limited) security of the English revolution, but the mellowness of the successful novelist who has looked the world in the face and doesn't care to go on looking. He turns to a loose and general cynicism:

> Ah! *Vanitas Vanitatum!* Which of us is happy in this world? Which of us has his desire? or, having it, is satisfied?—Come, children, let us shut up the box and the puppets, for our play is played out.[12]

It is the feeblest of endings, the flattest of statements of faith. And one doesn't even feel that Thackeray means it.

[12] *Ibid.*, Chap. LXVII.

On *Vanity Fair*

by Dorothy Van Ghent

Almost exactly a century separates *Tom Jones* from *Vanity Fair;*
but with *Vanity Fair,* so far as technical developments in the novel
are concerned, it is as if there had been none. We are in the story
telling convention of the "omniscient author" sanctioned by Fielding's great example, but with a damaging difference that is due,
not so much to an inherent inadequacy of that convention itself,
as the spiritual incoherency of another age. It is true that the technique of omniscient authorship can allow a relaxed garrulity—what
James called "the terrible fluidity of self-revelation"—for if the
author can enter the story in his own voice, there is nothing to
keep him from talking. After discussing Becky's adolescent designs
on Jos Sedley, and her visions of shawls and necklaces and aristocratic company which she imagines will be the rewards of marriage
with Jos, Thackeray comments,

> Charming Alnaschar visions! it is the happy privilege of youth to
> construct you, and many a fanciful young creature besides Rebecca
> Sharp has indulged in these delightful day-dreams ere now!

The comment is both inane and distracting—distracting our attention from the tense mental operations of Becky and turning it upon
the momentarily flaccid mentality of her author. The effect is one
of rather surprised irritation, as it is again when, having described
Jos's wardrobe, his pains in dressing, his vanity and shyness,
Thackeray remarks,

> If Miss Rebecca can get the better of *him,* and at her first entrance into
> life, she is a young person of no ordinary cleverness.

What we feel is that two orders of reality are clumsily getting in
each other's way: the order of imaginative reality, where Becky lives,

"*On* Vanity Fair." *From* The English Novel: Form and Function *by Dorothy
Van Ghent (New York: Holt, Rinehart & Winston, Inc., 1953), pp. 139–52.
Copyright 1953 by Dorothy Van Ghent. Reprinted by permission of the publisher.*

and the order of historical reality, where William Makepeace
Thackeray lives. The fault becomes more striking in the following
unforgivable parenthesis. Jos has just presented Amelia with flowers.

"Thank you, dear Joseph," said Amelia, quite ready to kiss her
brother, if he were so minded. (And I think for a kiss from such a
dear creature as Amelia, I would purchase all Mr. Lee's conservatories
out of hand.)

The picture of Thackeray himself kissing Amelia pulls Amelia
quite out of the created world of *Vanity Fair* and drops her into
some shapeless limbo of Thackerayan sentiment where she loses all
aesthetic orientation.

Nevertheless, the conventions employed in a work of art cannot
fairly be judged by themselves; they can be judged only as instru-
mental to a vision. The time in which Thackeray wrote was, compared with Fielding's time, itself looser in what we might call cul-
tural composition; its values were less integrated in a common
philosophical "style" or tenor of mind. In *Tom Jones,* the convention of the author's appearance in his book as "gregarious eye,"
stage manager, and moralist, is a strategy that is used with a
highly formal regularity of rhythm, and it animates every turn of
Fielding's language, as the ironic life of the language. Most important, the convention had benefited by an age's practice of and
belief in form, form in manners and rhetoric and politics and
philosophy—that is, by an age's coherently structured world view.
The set of feelings and ideas of which Fielding acts as vehicle, when
he makes his personal appearances in his book, is a set of feelings
and ideas with the stamp of spiritual consistency upon them. They
do not afflict us with a sense of confused perspectives between the
author's person and his work, his opinions and his creation, as do
Thackeray's. Whereas Thackeray seems merely to be victimized or
tricked by his adopted convention into a clumsy mishandling of
perspectives, Fielding manipulates the same convention deliberately
to produce displacements of perspective as an organic element of
composition. This is not to say that Fielding's creative perceptions
are, on the whole, more penetrating and profound than Thackeray's; indeed, Thackeray's seem to reach a good deal deeper into
the difficulties, compromises, and darkness of the human estate;
but Fielding's have the organizing power to make an ancient oral
convention of storytelling an appropriate instrument of his vision,
whereas the same convention—actually one that is most sympathetic
to Thackeray's gift of easy, perspicacious, ranging talk—becomes

a personal convenience for relaxation of aesthetic control, *even a means to counterfeit* his creative vision.

Becky ruminates, "I think I could be a good woman if I had five thousand a year," and adds with a sigh,

> "Heigho! I wish I could exchange my position in society, and all my relations, for a snug sum in the Three per Cent. Consols."

Here she is as true to herself psychologically as is Moll Flanders; but she is more complex than Moll, and we know perfectly that, at this promising stage in her career, the sigh is only a casual fantasy—arising chiefly out of boredom with the tedious business of cultivating the good graces of people much less intelligent than herself—and that if the "snug sum" were offered, she would not really exchange her prospects for it, for her temperament is not at present to be satisfied with snugness. There are to be pearl necklaces, presentation at court, a *succès fou* at Gaunt House. But Thackeray interprets for us.

> It may, perhaps, have struck her that to have been honest and humble, to have done her duty, and to have marched straightforward on her way, would have brought her as near happiness as that path by which she was striving to attain it.

This is a doctrine with which, in principle, we have no cause either to agree or disagree; a novel is not made of doctrines and principles, but of concretely imagined life, and whatever moral principle may be honestly adduced from that life must be intrinsic to it, concretely qualitative within it. *Vanity Fair* is strong with life, but in those concretions where it is alive there is nothing to suggest that to be "honest and humble" can possibly bring happiness. Becky is the happiest person in the book; she is alive from beginning to end, alive in intelligence and activity and *joie de vivre,* whether she is throwing Dr. Johnson's dictionary out of a coach window, in superb scorn of the humiliations of the poor, or exercising her adulterous charm on General Tufto, whether she is prancing to court to be made an "honest woman" (in stolen lace), or hiding a cognac bottle in a sordid bed. From Becky's delighted exercise in being alive, we can learn nothing about the happiness to be derived from humble dutifulness. On the other hand, from Amelia's humble dutifulness we can learn nothing that convinces us doctrinally that happiness lies in such a way of life. For it is not only that the brisk gait and vivid allure of Becky's egoistic and aggressive way of life make

Amelia look tepid, tear sodden, and compromised: this effect would not occur if the book were soundly structured, if its compositional center (what James called the "commanding centre" of the composition) were entirely firm and clear.

The actually functioning compositional center of *Vanity Fair* is that node or intersection of extensive social and spiritual relationships constituted by Becky's activities: her relationships with a multitude of individuals—Jos and Amelia and George, old Sir Pitt and Rawdon and Miss Crawley and the Bute Crawleys and the Pitt Crawleys, Lady Bareacres, Lord Steyne, and so on—and, through these individuals, her relationships with large and significant blocks of a civilization: with the middle-class Sedley block, that block which is in the process of physical destruction because of its lack of shrewdness in an acquisitive culture; with the other middle-class Osborne block, that block which has displaced the Sedley block through its own acquisitive shrewdness and through the necessarily accompanying denial of the compassionate and sympathetic human impulses; with the aristocratic Crawley block, in all its complexity of impotence and mad self-destruction, and (in young Sir Pitt, with the "gooseberry eyes") canny self-renovation through connivance with the economy and morality of the dominant middle class; with the ambiguous Steyne block, that is above the economic strife and therefore free of conventional moral concerns, but in its social freedom, "stained" deeply in nerves and blood. (In the names he gives people, Thackeray plays—like many novelists—on punning suggestion, as he does in the name of the crawling Crawleys, "raw-done" Rawdon, Sharp, Steyne, O'Dowd, etc.) This social relationship, concretized through Becky's relationship with individuals, is the hub of the book's meanings, its "compositional center." But beside this violently whirling and excited center is another, a weak and unavailing epicenter, where Amelia weeps and suffers and wins—wins Dobbin and solvency and neighborhood prestige and a good middle-class house with varnished staircases. Organized around the two centers are two plots, which have as little essentially to do with each other as Thackeray's creative imagination had to do with his sentimental, morally fearful reflections. He cannot bear to allow the wonderfully animated vision of Becky's world to speak for itself, for its meaning is too frightening; he must add to it a complementary world—Amelia's—to act as its judge and corrector. One thinks, in comparison, of Balzac, who was writing almost contemporaneously. Balzac was both as skeptical and as sentimental as Thackeray, but he was a passionate rationalist as well, and a much bolder dramatic formalist. In Balzac, the weak and the suffering and the pure in heart do not win. They have no pretensions to effective moral dynamism in the evil Balzacian world, which uses them as illustrative examples of the impotence of an "honest and humble" way of life.

As the convention of the omniscient author allows Thackeray to keep up a maladroit "sound track" of personal interpolations, so it also collaborates with his confusion as to where the compositional center of his book lies; for though the Becky-world and the Amelia-world, having no common motivation, confront each other with closed entrances, so to speak, yet the author is able, by abuse of his rights of omniscience, to move facilely through these closed doors. We assume that, in Thackeray's plan, the compositional center of the book was to be the moral valence between the two worlds. But there is no valence between them, nothing in either to produce a positive effect of significance on the other. The only effect is negative: the Amelia-plot pales into a morally immature fantasy beside the vivid life of the Becky-plot. For Becky is the great morally meaningful figure, the moral symbol, in the book, and beside her there is room and meaning for Amelia only as victim—certainly not as "success figure." The word "moral," which we have used rather frequently in these studies, needs perhaps a somewhat closer attention here. Becky is not virtuous, and in speaking of her as a morally significant figure, we cannot possibly confuse her moral meaning with the meaning of "virtue." She is a morally meaningful figure because she symbolizes the morality of her world at its greatest intensity and magnitude. The greediness that has only a reduced, personal meaning in Mrs. Bute Crawley, as she nags and blunders at old Miss Crawley's deathbed, acquires, through Becky's far more intelligent and courageous greed—as she encounters international techniques for the satisfaction of greed with her own subtle and knowing and superior techniques—an extensive social meaning. The corruption that, in old Sir Pitt, has meaning at most for the senility of a caste, becomes, in Becky's prostitution and treason and murderousness, the moral meaning of a culture. For Becky's activities are designed with intelligent discrimination and lively intuition, and they are carried through not only with unflagging will power but with joy as well. By representing her world at its highest energetic potential, by alchemizing all its evil but stupid and confused or formless impulses into brilliantly controlled intention, she endows her world with meaning. The meaning is such as to inspire horror; but the very fact that we conceive this horror intellectually and objectively is an acknowledgment of Becky's morally symbolic stature.

There is a French criticism of the English novel, that, in the English novel's characteristic concern with the social scene, it fails to explore "the deeper layers of personality." One understands the motivation of this criticism, if one compares representative French and English novels of approximately the same periods, although the criticism itself does not seem to be well thought out. *The Pilgrim's Progress* is populated with social "types," sparsely limned sketches that isolate certain traits, whereas, almost contemporaneously, Madame de Lafayette's *La Princesse de Clèves* is concentrated upon a depth illumination of the tortured psyche of a delicate woman who, in a loveless marriage, is moved by an illicit passion. Even *Clarissa Harlowe*, which is commonly thought of as an exhaustive representation of a young woman's emotions, is, because of its mythical qualities, rather more of a vision into the social soul than into that of a credible individual; and the difference is brought out by comparison with the almost contemporaneous *Manon Lescaut*, by the Abbé Prevost, in which the subject has certain affinities with that of *Clarissa* (except that it is the girl, here, who is the libertine, and the young man who is the afflicted one), but which is again—like so many French novels—a concentrated depth drawing of personal psychology rather than a social vision. One could pursue a number of other examples in the same way. But the difference is a relative difference only. For the "deeper layers of personality" are meaningless unless they can be related, at least by inference, to aspects of life that have some social generality; while social life is meaningless unless it finds embodiment in individuals. A more significant difference between classical French novels and classical English novels is one of method. The English novel has tended traditionally to symbolize certain phases of personality through the concrete image (Christian as the "man in rags" with a burden on his back; the Philosopher Square standing among Molly's "other female utensils" when the curtain falls in the bedroom; Clarissa, with streaming eyes and disheveled bosom, prostrating herself before Lovelace; Jaggers washing his hands or Miss Havisham beside the rotten bridecake); while the French novel has tended traditionally to a discursive analysis of feeling and motive, as has the French drama. Image and analysis are merely two different ways of mirroring what goes on in the soul. The methods are never exclusive; and we find such significant exceptions to the general tendency as Flaubert's *Madame Bovary*, where the image dominates, and Conrad's *Lord Jim*, where analysis dominates.

Let us illustrate, from *Vanity Fair*, the method of the image and what it is able to imply as to the "deeper layers of personality." Characteristically, in this book, the social concern is paramount. We have spoken of the various "blocks" of this civilization, some slipping into rubble by the crush of the others or by internal decay, some thrusting themselves up by the neighboring defaultment. But governing all the movements is one ethos of aggressive egoism, articulated through the acquisition of cash and through the prestige fantasies born of cash. Becky herself is a member of no particular class and confined to no particular "block." (Significantly, she is the daughter of a Bohemian artist and a French music-hall singer.) She is more mobile than any of the other characters, because of her freedom from caste, and thus is able to enter into a great variety of class relationships: this is the peculiar novelistic virtue of the picara and picaro, and the enduring source of virility of the pica-resque form—the protagonist's freedom of movement. Still acting under the same ethos as that governing the whole civilization, Becky is able to represent its tendencies without class pretenses. Thus Becky, like Moll Flanders, though a strongly individualized character, is the type of a whole civilization, a small-scale model of a world, a microcosm in which the social macrocosm is subtilized and intensified and made significant. With this predominantly social bearing of the novel, the characters—even Becky—tend to be depicted in a relatively "external" way: that is, there is relatively little discussion of the nuances of their feelings and their motivations; they are not self-analytical characters, as characters in French novels tend to be, nor do they spend much time in deliberate analysis of each other; they appear to us physically, in action; and —with some generalized interpretive help from the author himself (whose interpretations, as we have noted, we cannot always trust) —we enter into their motives and states of feeling by our own intuition. Examples are manifold. There is Becky's meeting of George's eyes in the mirror as she and Amelia, Jos and George, are leaving for Vauxhall: a flashing, accidental illumination of his vanity and vulnerability—and though here might be an excellent opportunity for Becky to engage in psychological speculations and deliberations, little of the kind occurs. There is the physical flash, the illumination by image only, and Becky has George's number. And yet later, when George and Amelia, Becky and Rawdon, meet on their honeymoon trips at Brighton, and Becky with almost unconscious slyness encourages George to make love to her, the early image of the meeting of eyes in a mirror plays on the reader's understanding of motivation, as it does again when we see Becky in overt sexual aggressiveness at the Brussels ball. There has been no need of discursive analysis of motive; the image does the work.

Or—another instance of the work of the image—there is Jos, in his obesity and his neckcloths and his gorgeous waistcoats. We should not expect Jos to analyze himself, nor anyone else to have an interest in analyzing what he feels, for he is below the level of what is rationally interesting; and yet, from the physical picture alone, we are made intuitively aware of deeply disturbed "layers of personality" in Jos. He is one of the most complicated psychological portraits in the book (more complicated, for instance, than that of another voluptuary, the Marquis of Steyne, who has more refined opportunities than Jos and a better head), extremely unpleasant, with suggestions of impalpable submerged perversities, pathetic, with a pathos that is at the same time an outrage to our feeling for what is humanly cognizable in pathos—for Jos is a glandularly suffering animal, with the "human" so hidden in his tortured fat that we feel it to be obscene, while we must still recognize it as human. Jos offering his neck to Isidore's razor . . . is a complex image of a kind of fear so muddied, an image of a psychological state so profoundly irrational, that we react to it with an impulse of horrified laughter—the intuitive horror having no other outlet than in a sense of the absurd. At the same time that these physical images of Jos flash to the mind's eye an impression of something deep and possible in individual personality, they are made by Thackeray to represent to the social reason an extremely significant phase of a culture. We see in Jos's obesity the sickness of a culture, the sickness due to spiritual gourmandism, or, in simpler but still metaphorical words, to "overeating"; in his shyness of women, the repressions and abnormalities of a sick culture; in his stupidity and febrile conceit, the intellectual numbing and tubercular euphoria of a culture. Thus the physical image, here, mirrors most fearful depths of the personal and, at the same time, most threatening perspectives of the social life.

We shall cite a few more illustrations of this method of the "image," as Thackeray uses it, keeping in mind its double significance, its significance for personal psychology (the "deeper layers of personality") and its social significance. But in preparation for these particular citations, we should speak of one singularly important theme of *Vanity Fair*, and that is a theme which

we shall call the theme of the "fathers." In the eighteenth-century
novels that we have read, the "father" has appeared in a light that
is rather different from the light that is thrown on the "father" in
nineteenth-century novels. There is Squire Allworthy, for instance,
who, as "father," though he may have his failures of insight, is
still an affirmative moral reference in the *Tom Jones* system of
values; he is idealized, but this itself is significant of the fact that
the "father" still represents a moral ideal. In the eighteenth century, the idea of the "father" was not, on the whole, ambiguous, or
suggestive of doubts or deficiencies or culpability—that is, as this
idea is reflected in literature. Mr. Harlowe, in *Clarissa,* is the most
exceptional example; but even here, the daughter's return to her
"Father's house," on the elevated stage of the divine, is an affirmation and sanction of the usual parental-filial relationship of authority and obedience which is esteemed to be universally valid; Mr.
Harlowe made a mistake, but so did Clarissa make a mistake; in-
formed by Clarissa's passion, it is to be hoped that no other
daughters or fathers will ever make such mistakes. In *Tristram
Shandy,* the "father," Walter Shandy, is a freak, yet he is presented
only under the aspect of general human freakishness, pleasant and
interesting eccentricity, and we are led in no way to think of him
in terms of parental culpability; indeed, as "father," he takes his
responsibility most enormously—to be the right kind of father and
to bring up the right kind of son are his devouring concern; the
inquiries and devotions of fatherhood—as to conditions of conception, size of the son's nose, the son's name, his education—form
the whole shape of Walter Shandy's mental activities, his very eccentricity. Similarly in Smollett's *Humphry Clinker,* where the
"father" (an uncle, in this case) is a querulous hypochondriac,
leading his life in a tone of objection to everything, we are "on his
side," we object when he objects, with a grain of salt for his
elderly fury; and the book has its moral equipoise in the rightness
of this "father's" perceptions.

We see, in the notion of the father in eighteenth-century literature, a reflection of social trust: of trust in and reliance upon and
devotion to a general social system of values—that coherent "world
view" of the eighteenth century that we have spoken of earlier in
this essay. For, under our anciently inherited patriarchal organization of the family, an organization that inevitably extended itself
into political organization and philosophic organization, the "fa-
ther-imago" has acquired vast symbolic extension beyond domestic
life and into general social life: our "fathers" are not only our

individual fathers but all those who have come before us—society as it has determined our conditions of existence and the problems we have to confront. *Vanity Fair,* with its panorama of western European international society as backdrop to the heroine's activities, is full of "fathers," sick fathers, guilty fathers.

Curiously enough, we have seen the inception of the theme of the "fathers" in Jane Austen, despite her eighteenth-century social sensibility; and it is—along with her inception of modern technique in the handling of the "point of view"—a striking mark of her modernity. In *Pride and Prejudice,* the father, Mr. Bennet, is anything but the morally idealized figure of Squire Allworthy; and even as an "eccentric" or "humorous" character (in the older sense), he casts moral shadows that, for instance, Walter Shandy —another "eccentric"—does not cast. Mr. Bennet, as father, is guilty. In Dickens' *Great Expectations,* we have seen that the theme of the "father" dominates the meanings of the book, and we have seen how many inflections Dickens is able to get out of this theme. Crossing language boundaries, we find in Stendhal's *The Red and the Black* (1830) various implementations of the same theme: Julien's revolt against the peasant grossness of his own father, and his finding of a "spiritual father" in a Jansenist monk, who himself is under suspicion from the religious institution to which he belongs (here the father who is worthy of respect is himself virtually a social outcast). In Balzac's *Père Goriot*—whose title is indicative of the "father" theme—the actual father, Goriot, is a degenerate victim of corrupt social ideas, while the "spiritual father" of the hero is an out-and-out criminal. Turgenev's *Fathers and Sons* announces the same theme by its title; and again here the "fathers" are inadequate. In Dostoevski's *The Brothers Karamazov,* the sons' murder of the father is the focus of plot, and we have the famous question, on the part of Ivan Karamazov, "Who doesn't desire his father's death?" The title of D. H. Lawrence's *Sons and Lovers* indicates again the modern preoccupation with the parental-filial relationship. Joyce's *Portrait of the Artist* and his *Ulysses* carry out the same preoccupation: in the former, the hero's actual father goes to pieces and the family disintegrates with him; in the latter, the hero's "spiritual father" is a Jew, emotionally an alien in the Dublin of the book, without integration with the social body, and as lost and wandering as the son.

It is significant of the vital intuitiveness of Thackeray's *Vanity Fair* that the theme of the "fathers" should have such importance: in this book, an immensely impressive female, herself quite father-

less, manages to articulate in her career the most meaningful
social aspects of the "father" theme. We need, in this view of the
book, to free ourselves from the narrower Freudian aspects of the
theme and to think in terms of Thackeray's broad social perspective, where the "fathers" are such variants as Mr. Sedley,
Mr. Osborne, old Sir Pitt, even the Marquis of Steyne: in other
words, such variants as to include all the older, authoritative, and
determinative aspects of society.

And now, with this general notion of the significance of the
theme of parental authority, we can consider what Thackeray
manages to get out of the "image" of old Mr. Osborne and his
daughters coming down the stairs, in their evening ritual, to
dinner.

> The obedient bell in the lower regions began ringing the announce-
> ment of the meal. The tolling over, the head of the family thrust his
> hands into the great tail-pockets of his great blue coat and brass but-
> tons, and without waiting for a further announcement, strode down-
> stairs alone, scowling over his shoulder at the four females.
>
> "What's the matter now, my dear?" asked one of the other, as they
> rose and tripped gingerly behind the sire.
>
> "I suppose the funds are falling," whispered Miss Wirt; and so,
> trembling and in silence, this hushed female company followed their
> dark leader.

In the lines just before this there is one other, inconspicuous,
touch: in the drawing room where they are waiting for dinner is
a chronometer "surmounted by a cheerful brass group of the
sacrifice of Iphigenia." The depths which are suggested by this
picture, but quite as if accidentally, are the depths of Greek
tragedy and, still further back, of Freud's dim, sub-human, imagined
"primitive horde": the "dark leader" with his "hushed female
company," and the ridiculous but furious Victorian clock "cheer-
fully" symbolizing the whole. Antiquity's dark brooding over the
monstrous nature of man is made to take on, in this incidental
image of a family's going to dinner, the unwholesomeness and
perversity that have been added to man's classical monstrosity by
"falling funds," a drop in the stock market.

There is the recurrent incident in the hall outside the bedroom
where old Miss Crawley is sick, Becky tending her, everyone—
including Becky—waiting for and speculating on the "reversionary
spoils."

> Captain Rawdon got an extension of leave on his aunt's illness, and
> remained dutifully at home. He was always in her ante-chamber. (She

lay sick in the state bedroom into which you entered by the little blue
saloon.) His father was always meeting him there; or if he came down
the corridor ever so quietly, his father's door was sure to open, and
the hyaena face of the old gentleman to glare out. What was it set one
to watch the other so? A generous rivalry, no doubt, as to which should
be most attentive to the dear sufferer in the state bedroom. Rebecca
used to come out and comfort both of them—or one or the other of
them rather.

Short and unemphasized as the passage is (outside of one ironic
line, it consists only of an image, the image of Rawdon opening
a door and looking into the corridor, of the old man's "hyaena
face" instantly looking out from an opposite door, of Becky
coming down the hall to "comfort" them), it contains a pregnant
and disturbing meaning, both for personal psychology and for
social psychology. Later, when Becky will attempt to inform Sir
Pitt about her clandestine marriage, but without telling him the
name of her husband, he will be uproariously amused; but as
soon as she tells him the name—his son, Rawdon—he goes mad
with inexplicable fury. We look back mentally to the incidents
in the hall outside Miss Crawley's sickroom, where son and father
glare at each other, and where Becky comes to comfort them
separately, holding each in suspense as to her amorous favor. And
we look forward also to that horrible line in Becky's letter to
Rawdon (after the disclosure to Sir Pitt), where she says, "I
might have been somebody's mamma, instead of—Oh, I tremble,
I tremble . . ." What is contained here is probably the most
excruciatingly primitive father-son battle in literature, with one
of the most sensitively feminine but perversely sentimental reflections upon it. How are we to say, in such a case, whether what
we are observing is the "deeper layers of personality" or the social
scene?

And then there is the description of the turmoil surrounding
old Sir Pitt's death. It consists of a succession of images: Miss
Horrocks flitting in ribbons through "the halls of their fathers";
again Miss Horrocks

> of the guilty ribbons, with a wild air, trying at the presses and escri-
> toires with a bunch of keys.—

while upstairs they are "trying to bleed" Sir Pitt (the "trying to"
suggests unknown but repulsive derangements); the servant girl
screaming and making faces at him in private while he whimpers.
The cumulation of these images, scattered and casual as they are,

makes the face of a gorgon of destiny. The personal and social idea of the "father" (an idea which is inextricably both personal and social) is made the nasty companion of the ribbon-flitting Miss Horrocks; when Sir Pitt gives the family pearls to Lady Jane ("Pretty pearls—never gave 'em to the ironmonger's daughter"), marital relationships, with all they mean for the security created for us by our elders, are referred back retrospectively to Sir Pitt's chronic tipsiness and Lady Crawley's worsted knitting—an "enormous interminable piece of knitting"—

> She worked that worsted day and night . . . She had not character enough to take to drinking . . . ;

drawers are tried while the "father" is bled; and finally—so great is the prestige of this "father" and baronet—the servant girl has full amplitude to scream obscenities and make faces at him, for he has turned into "a whimpering old idiot put in and out of bed and cleaned and fed like a baby."

The burden of Thackeray's intuition into personal psychology and its social meaning falls on images like these, and they are innumerable in *Vanity Fair*. But the greatness of *Vanity Fair* is not in scattered images, sensitive as these are. They are all gathered up in Becky Sharp. Becky does for Jos, murderously, at the end; and what she does to Jos is only cancerously implicit in himself and the civilization that has made him; she is the darkness—shining obsidianly in an intelligent personality—in old Mr. Osborne's dense sadism against his daughters and his corruption of the meaning of paternal responsibility toward his son; she manipulates the insane father-son conflict between Sir Pitt and Rawdon; and she is the "guilty ribbons" of Miss Horrocks (instead of a servant's ribbons she has a courtesan's pearls) and at the same time the whimpering idiocy of the dying Sir Pitt (paralleling his repulsive attack of mortality, she inflicts a similarly repulsive mortality on Jos)—for she is at once all the imperatively aggressive, insanely euphoric impulses of a morally sick civilization, and an individual condensation of that civilization. We question whether we would understand her at all, or be charmed by her buoyancy or appalled by her destructiveness, if her impulses were not memorabilia of our own and her civilization our heritage.

Vanity Fair

by Kathleen Tillotson

Thackeray turns away, then, from heroes and heroines, from the conventional ending, from the "professional parts of novels." And he evades the contemporary categories: *Vanity Fair* is not a novel of low life (its lowest level is the apartments at Fulham, or —unexpectedly—the elder Sir Pitt's *ménage* in Great Gaunt Street), nor of high life (the highest level is the ball at Gaunt House, which would contain some surprises for the devotees of Mrs. Gore);[1] it is not a military novel, despite Waterloo, nor a domestic novel, despite the number of family scenes. It is not historical, although it is a novel about the past; the period in which it is set is robbed of its usual glamour, and the past is strangely interpenetrated by the present. Thackeray's preface, "Before the Curtain," illustrates his almost malicious way of teasing expectation:

> There are scenes of all sorts; some of dreadful combats, some grand and lofty horse-riding, some scenes of high life, some of very middling indeed: some love-making for the sentimental, and some light comic business; the whole accompanied by appropriate scenery, and brilliantly illuminated by the Author's own candles.

He promises variety; but he also gives unity, and not only by the continuous presence of the "author's own candles." The principles of organization in *Vanity Fair* must next be considered: the positive truth which Thackeray substitutes for the conventions of fiction.

"Vanity Fair." *From* Novels of the Eighteen-Forties *by Kathleen Tillotson* (Oxford: Clarendon Press, 1954), pp. 234–56. Copyright 1954 by Kathleen Tillotson. Reprinted by permission of the author and publisher. Section 1 is omitted.

[1] Mrs. Procter said, "He has avoided the two extremes in which so many of our popular writers delight" (*The Letters and Private Papers of William Makepeace Thackeray*, ed. Gordon N. Ray, 4 vols. [Cambridge, Mass., 1945–46] II, 313).

By choosing as his field "the debatable land between the middle classes and the aristocracy" [2] he takes a social area which, though less extensive than Dickens's, gives him considerable vertical range. All the characters are seen in relation to "society," living in it or on it; for each character he defines the rung on the ladder, the place on the slippery slope, the rocky ledge where they hang by finger-tips. None are unplaced; which means that the "other nation" is excluded—it was not beyond his ken, but he chose to ignore it here.

There is less scope for oddity than in Dickens's world, for Vanity Fair is a world in which it is important to conform. Those who give up the pretence of conformity, like Sir Pitt Crawley or Lord Steyne, show that Thackeray can provide his own grotesques, with only the monstrosity which actual life provides. Specific comparison with Dickens illustrates Thackeray's different attitude to reality: the observed reality is often the same, but Thackeray mines into it, where Dickens makes it a springboard into fantasy. Even in his names Thackeray wishes "to convey the sentiment of reality." Dickens's may be actual, but they are chosen for their oddity and comic appropriateness, while Thackeray masks his satire in plausibility, preferring a subtle suggestiveness; as in "Steyne," with its pun and its relation to Regency Brighton; or the contrast, rich in association, of the liquid and romantic "Amelia Sedley" with the hinted racial astuteness of "Rebecca Sharp."

Thackeray's characters exist in a denser context than perhaps any characters in fiction. They are aware of past time; they draw on childhood memories.

> "Am I much better to do now in the world than I was when I was the poor painter's daughter, and wheedled the grocer round the corner for sugar and tea? Suppose I had married Francis who was so fond of me. . . ." [3]

It is the only time we ever hear of "Francis." In the shadow, just beyond every character, but ready to catch the spotlight for a single instant when needed, seem to be all the people the character has ever met. Here is the sole appearance of Edward Dale:

> the junior of the house, who purchased the spoons for the firm, was, in fact, very sweet upon Amelia, and offered for her in spite of all.

[2] Review-article by W. C. Roscoe in *National Review* (January 1856); collected in *Poems and Essays* (2 vols., 1860).
[3] Ch. xli.

He married Miss Louisa Cutts (daughter of Higham and Cutts, the
eminent corn-factors) with a handsome fortune in 1820; and is now
living in splendour, and with a numerous family, at his elegant
villa, Muswell Hill.[4]

Odd corners of their houses, or possessions, may similarly light up
at a touch. Their ancestries and family histories may be given;
the baptismal names of the Crawley ancestors, according well with
their surname, epitomize the political vanities of two centuries.
And no single paragraph about Lord Steyne tells us more about
him and his society, or about vanity in high places, than that
list of titles and honours in his "obituary":

> the Most Honourable George Gustavus, Marquis of Steyne, Earl of
> Gaunt and of Gaunt Castle, in the Peerage of Ireland, Viscount
> Hellborough, Baron Pitchley and Grillsby, a Knight of the Most
> Noble Order of the Garter, of the Golden Fleece of Spain, of the
> Russian Order of Saint Nicholas of the First Class, of the Turkish
> Order of the Crescent, First Lord of the Powder Closet and Groom
> of the Back Stairs, Colonel of the Gaunt or Regent's Own Regiment
> of Militia, a Trustee of the British Museum, an Elder Brother of
> the Trinity House, a Governor of the White Frairs, and D.C.L. . . .[5]

Such fullness of documentation, never introduced heavily, but
ready to be drawn on where it is needed, is significant of Thackeray's emphasis on character in its social relations. This has
been noted by all his critics, and best defined by Brownell:

> Thackeray's personages are never portrayed in isolation. They are
> part of the *milieu* in which they exist, and which has itself therefore
> much more distinction and relief than an environment which is
> merely a framework. How they regard each other, how they feel
> toward and what they think of each other, the mutuality of their
> very numerous and vital relations, furnishes an important strand in
> the texture of the story in which they figure. Their activities are
> modified by the air they breathe in common. Their conduct is
> controlled, their ideas affected, even their desires and ambitions
> dictated, by the general ideas of the society that includes them.[6]

But it would be wrong to see Thackeray as a fatalist about character. That Becky believes she might have been a good woman
on five thousand a year is itself part of her character ("Becky

[4] Ch. xvii.
[5] Ch. lxiv.
[6] W. C. Brownell, *Victorian Prose Masters* (1902), p. 29.

consoled herself . . .");[7] some virtues may be accidental, but "circumstance only brings out the latent defect or quality, and does not create it." [8] Thackeray is not optimistic enough about human nature (less so, for example, than George Eliot) to have much belief in the power of people to change themselves:

> We alter very little. . . . Our mental changes are like our grey hairs and our wrinkles—but the fulfilment of the plan of mortal growth and decay.[9]

His characters are so mixed, so often on a moral borderland, so subject to time, and also so gradually unfolded—often with unpredictable detail—that they do not give the impression of being static. But they are not shown as evolving, nor do they undergo much inward conflict; and so the unity given to a novel by dominating or developing characters is not found. Only one of Thackeray's novels—*Pendennis*—is even formally built upon the fortunes of a single character; and Arthur Pendennis is less an interesting individual than a nineteenth-century variant of Everyman.

* * *

Without recourse to obvious devices, without a hero or heroine or any single central figure, without any "inward" study of development in character, Thackeray nevertheless makes us feel *Vanity Fair* a unity. This has sometimes been underestimated, and the novel apologized for as loose, rambling, and casual, though admitted to be rich and comprehensive: the apology may even lay the blame on the serial form. But the serial novel, serially written, is . . . really the less likely to be loose and rambling; only some degree of forethought makes such writing even possible; and the reader's interest, spread over a year and a half, will not be held unless there is a genuine continuity and a firm centre of interest. It is a contention of this whole study that both novelists and critics of this time were interested in "unity"; we may recall that Lytton claimed that "composition" should be recognized in novels as in paintings, and *Fraser's* critic of 1851 says firmly:

> One of the great achievements . . . in the art of the novelist is unity. If we cannot get that, the next best thing is progress.[10]

[7] Ch. xli.
[8] *Pendennis*, ch. lix; and cf. *Esmond*, Book II, ch. i.
[9] *Pendennis*, ch. lix.
[10] *Fraser's* (October 1851), p. 382.

A more reputable critical view, one indeed that is insidiously tempting, is that Thackeray's formal purpose is a "picture" of society. This view, so persuasively set forth in Lubbock's *Craft of Fiction,* does admit of composition, even if "picture" is extended to "panorama"; but it accounts only for a part of *Vanity Fair.* For it allows too little for our fascinated sense of progression; too little also for Thackeray the moralist.

The clear and obvious line of progression in the novel is surely also, when closely considered, the chief of its unities: that is, the converging and diverging, parallel and contrasting fortunes of the two girls, Rebecca Sharp and Amelia Sedley.[11] In narrative terms, the basis of the contrast is simple (the moral contrast, on the other hand, is ironic and complex); it is that Rebecca attempts actively to shape her own fortunes, while Amelia passively accepts hers. They begin with "the world before them," on their last day at Minerva House Academy in Chiswick Mall. Their manner of leaving Miss Pinkerton's differentiates them at the outset in character as well as social status. Rebecca is nineteen and Amelia sixteen, but Rebecca has never been a child (Thackeray refers early to her "dismal precocity") and Amelia is never to grow up. But throughout the first number (chapters i to iv) their similarity as well as difference is emphasized; both are occupied with the "vanity" of husband-hunting (the title of chapter ii is "In which Miss Sharp and Miss Sedley prepare to open the campaign"); Rebecca is laying her snares for Jos Sedley, Amelia sighing and smiling at George Osborne. In the closing number, after seventeen years, Amelia at last consents to forget George, and Rebecca at last has Jos inescapably in her toils. Throughout the narrative a balance of interest between Amelia and Rebecca is steadily maintained; in every number there is something of both, and when they are apart the juxtaposition of chapters defining the progress in their histories still forms a pattern. In Number V (chapters xv to xviii) Rebecca is thrown out of favour with the Crawleys when her marriage to Rawdon is revealed; Mr. Sedley has failed in business and George Osborne's defection is threatened, but there is a hopeful turn at the end to bring Amelia's marriage into sight and match the close of Number IV. In Number XIV (chapters xlvii to l) there is a simple contrast between the zenith of Becky's fortunes (presented at Court, dining at Gaunt House) and

---

[11] The point has of course been made by several critics, from *Fraser's* (September 1848, p. 347) to our own day, but I think with insufficient sense of the subtlety of Thackeray's intentions.

the nadir of Amelia's (in poverty, and parted from her son). In Number XVI comes Becky's "fall," set beside the first hint of Amelia's "rise," the number closing with Dobbin's return from India (chapter lvi). There are also the subtler running contrasts of Becky's treatment of her son Rawdon, Amelia's of George: subtle, because Thackeray is critical both of heartless neglect and passionate possessiveness. Or the likeness within difference of Amelia's stupid fidelity to her husband's memory, and Becky's stupid infidelity to Rawdon. Each is an egoist; Thackeray's comment when Dobbin leaves Amelia is pointed:

> She didn't wish to marry him, but she wished to keep him. She wished to give him nothing, but that he should give her all. It is a bargain not unfrequently levied in love.[12]

Outside its context, the second of these sentences would be taken as describing Becky.

But the structural ironies are clearest when the two histories converge and entangle:

> [Becky] was thinking in her heart, "It was George Osborne who prevented my marriage."—And she loved George Osborne accordingly.[13]

Her small revenge of malicious teasing in chapter xiv (where these words are echoed) is the prelude to her triumph at Brussels:

> [George] was carrying on a desperate flirtation with Mrs. Crawley. He . . . passed his evenings in the Crawleys' company; losing money to the husband and flattering himself that the wife was dying in love for him. It is very likely that this worthy couple never absolutely conspired, and agreed together in so many words: the one to cajole the young gentleman, whilst the other won his money at cards: but they understood each other perfectly well. . . .[14]

At the ball on the night before Waterloo she receives his note "coiled like a snake among the flowers"—a note whose substance is not divulged until the closing number. The next day she visits the half-suspecting Amelia:

> Amelia . . . drew back her hand, and trembled all over. "Why are *you* here, Rebecca?" she said, still looking at her solemnly, with her large eyes. These glances troubled her visitor.

[12] Ch. lxvi.
[13] Ch. vi.
[14] Ch. xxix.

"She must have seen him give me the letter at the ball," Rebecca thought.

But Amelia's accusations are in general terms, and are so answered:

> "Amelia, I protest before God, I have done my husband no wrong," Rebecca said, turning from her.
> "Have you done *me* no wrong, Rebecca? You did not succeed, but you tried. Ask your heart if you did not?"
> She knows nothing, Rebecca thought.[15]

The number ends with George Osborne's death on the battle-field; from this mid-point in the novel proceed Amelia's simple subsequent fortunes—ten years of widowhood sentimentally faithful to a mythical memory, and resistance to Dobbin's suit. The two converge again when Amelia, abroad with Jos and Dobbin, meets Rebecca, now disgraced and outside the social pale, but resilient as ever. She renews her designs on Jos, and when Dobbin, at last despairing of Amelia, returns to England, finds Amelia in her way. She reproaches her for refusing Dobbin:

> "I tried—I tried my best, indeed I did, Rebecca," said Amelia deprecatingly, "but I couldn't forget—"; and she finished her sentence by looking up at the portrait.
> "Couldn't forget *him!*" cried out Becky, "that selfish humbug, that low-bred cockney dandy, that padded booby, who had neither wit, nor manners, nor heart. . . . He never cared for you. He used to sneer about you to me, time after time; and made love to me the week after he married you."
> "It's false! it's false! Rebecca," cried out Amelia, starting up.
> "Look there, you fool," Becky said, still with provoking good-humour, and taking a little paper out of her belt, she opened it and flung it into Emmy's lap. "You know his handwriting. He wrote that to me—wanted me to run away with him—gave it me under your nose, the day before he was shot—and served him right!" Becky repeated.[16]

Apparently then the wheel comes full circle: Becky ending as she began, as Amelia's friend. But Thackeray has one more surprise in store: the revelation is not decisive, for Amelia has already relented and written to recall Dobbin. The inner necessity of the scene is rather to leave no sham unexposed, and to keep our

[15] Ch. xxxi.
[16] Ch. lxvii.

moral attitude to the two "heroines" complicated to the last. For
Becky's is the true view of the case, and her action righteous,
though from mixed motives. But Amelia's actions, although mud-
dleheaded, are to the last motivated by love.

"Anyone who mistakes [Amelia] for a simple character has
missed *Vanity Fair*." [17] The mistake has been common, and has
in modern times taken the particularly silly form of regarding
Amelia as the straight representation of an ideal now outmoded.
But even apart from Thackeray's own view, writ large in phrase
after phrase, his contemporaries did not unanimously applaud
Amelia. Some went even too far in the other direction: "No
woman resents Rebecca . . . but every woman resents his selfish
and inane Amelia." [18] (It was perhaps more gratifying to the
woman of the eighteen-forties, and certainly rarer, to see herself
presented in fiction as a clever rogue than as an amiable fool.) If
Thackeray has an ideal in mind, then Amelia and Becky are both
far (though not equally far) removed from it; of the disproportion
between heart and brain possible to the feminine character they
provide extreme instances. Some readers may be more legitimately
misled by the necessary difference in treatment. The active Becky
can be displayed, where the suffering, yielding Amelia must be described. The tone of the description is deliberately ambiguous,
seeming often sentimentally protective, but with enough impatience
breaking through to show that the author wishes to confuse and
make fun of the sentimental reader. It is not necessary to attribute
confusion to Thackeray himself; there is room with such a character for genuine indulgence as well as impatience. Besides, he
has an ulterior, "literary" motive in Amelia: Becky is a wholly
new kind of heroine, Amelia the old kind ironically exposed. It
is possible that Amelia may sometimes be imperfectly disengaged
from "the unwritten part" of his novels, not quite free from her
moorings in his own emotional life;[19] whereas Becky swims free

[17] Brownell, op. cit., p. 31.
[18] Mrs. Jameson, as quoted by J. W. Dodds, *Thackeray* (1941), p. 130; Mrs.
Brookfield, and Thackeray's mother made similar comments.
[19] He told Mrs. Brookfield that she was "a piece of Amelia—My Mother is
another half: my poor little wife *y est pour beaucoup*" (30 June 1848; *Letters*,
II, 394). But it is difficult to take this seriously; the three women can have had
little in common with each other or with Amelia except charm and obstinacy.
Perhaps there is something of Jane Brookfield's faithfulness to a husband
Thackeray was coming to think unworthy of her. But J. Y. T. Greig, who has
pressed this interpretation furthest (in *Thackeray: A Reconsideration*, 1950)
seems to make his bricks of very little straw.

in the pure element of art.[20] Becky is one of those characters—
like Chaucer's Pardoner—who can fully engage our aesthetic
sympathies while defying most of our moral ones; Thackeray is
not less a moralist for allowing us to enjoy her as a spectacle, for
his judgement of her is firm. Her attraction is partly that of the
triumphant knave in a world of knaves and fools; enjoyment is
not complicated by pity for the less successful knaves, like the
younger Sir Pitt, nor yet for the fools, like Jos Sedley or even
Briggs; these belong to the world of satirical comedy, where we
have the freedom of feeling that "fools are responsible for their
folly." The comic inventiveness of these triumphs provides some
of the most brilliant flashes of the book:

> She listened with the tenderest kindly interest, sitting by him,
> and hemming a shirt for her dear little boy. Whenever Mrs. Rawdon
> wished to be particularly humble and virtuous, this little shirt
> used to come out of her work-box. It had got to be too small for
> Rawdon long before it was finished, though.[21]
> "How I have been waiting for you! Stop! not yet—in one minute
> you shall come in." In that instant she put a rouge-pot, a brandy-
> bottle, and a plate of broken meat into her bed. . . .
> . . . "I had but one child, one darling, one hope, one joy . . .
> and they tore it from me;" and she put her hand to her heart with
> a passionate gesture of despair, burying her face for a moment on the
> bed.
> The brandy-bottle inside clinked up against the plate which
> held the cold sausage.[22]

But Thackeray does not go too far in enlisting the reader's pleasure on the side of wickedness. For this he had criticized Bulwer
and Ainsworth:

> Don't let us have any juggling and thimble-rigging with virtue
> and vice, so that, at the end of three volumes, the bewildered
> reader shall not know which is which.[23]

For this he was even, unjustly, criticized himself: "Sin is fire; and
Mr. Thackeray makes fireworks of it." [24] But his judgement of
Becky never falters, and it is made plain to the reader through one

[20] There are two possible "originals" for Becky, Sydney Morgan and Theresa
Reviss; but they can have provided no more than the "germ of the real."
[21] Ch. xliv.
[22] Ch. lxv.
[23] *Catherine*, ch. i (*Works*, III, 31).
[24] Roscoe, loc. cit.

character in particular: Rawdon Crawley. The words in the "discovery" scene are pointed: "I am innocent," says Becky. "Was she guilty or not?" asks Thackeray, and apparently leaves it an open question. But the technical question is not the most relevant one: her essential guilt rests in Rawdon's simple accusation: "You might have spared me £100, Becky; I have always shared with you." The words take us back to the night before Waterloo, with Rawdon making his last dispositions—"my duelling pistols in rosewood case (same which I shot Captain Marker)"; and Becky stands condemned of cold-hearted treachery.

The relation of these two is one of the main sources of "progression" in the novel, and is worth tracing. "Rawdon's marriage," says Thackeray, "was one of the honestest actions which we shall have to record in any portion of that gentleman's biography." [25] Unlike George Osborne (the contrast is firmly indicated) he married for love; which puts him at an initial disadvantage with Becky, who married him in hopes of his aunt's money.

> Is his case a rare one? and don't we see every day in the world many an honest Hercules at the apron-strings of Omphale, and great whiskered Samsons prostrate in Dalilah's lap? [26]

Becky's contempt is masked at first:

> "If he had but a little more brains," she thought to herself, "I might make something of him;" but she never let him perceive the opinion she had of him. . . .[27]

But not masked for long; not when Miss Crawley's favour seems again within reach:

> "You fool! you ought to have gone in, and never come out again," Rebecca said.
> "Don't call me names," said the big guardsman, sulkily. "Perhaps I *was* a fool, Becky, but you shouldn't say so." [28]

Their relation is fully and picturesquely defined in the farewell scene before Waterloo; but its deterioration is also hinted, in the narrative that so lightly sketches the "three or four years" [29] which follow. At first, Rawdon's illusions are still intact; "He believed

[25] Ch. xvi.
[26] Ch. xvi.
[27] Ch. xvii.
[28] Ch. xxv.
[29] Chs. xxxiv, xxxvi, and xxxvii.

in his wife as much as the French soldiers in Napoleon"; and with as little grounds. We are left to infer that, his aunt having died and left him only £100, Rawdon is no longer an investment worth nursing. Becky is flying at higher game. The scene that marks the change is of the kind that lights up far more than itself: the evening scene in Curzon Street, Becky in the centre of a party of gentlemen including Lord Steyne. (It is our first introduction to Lord Steyne; Thackeray's method is to make us feel that he has been there a long time.) Rawdon is "sitting silent without the circle," engaged in "shearing a Southdown." The closing words mark the grouping as typical:

> "How is Mrs. Crawley's husband," Lord Steyne used to say by way of a good day when they met; and indeed that was now his avocation in life. He was Colonel Crawley no more. He was Mrs. Crawley's husband. . . .
>
> "Hang it, I ain't clever enough for her—I know it. She won't miss me," he used to say: and he was right: his wife did not miss him.
>
> Rebecca was fond of her husband. She was always perfectly good-humoured and kind to him. She did not even show her scorn much for him; perhaps she liked him the better for being a fool. He was her upper servant and *maître d'hôtel*.

Two years later he is "more and more isolated every day . . . beat and cowed into laziness and submission. Dalilah had imprisoned him and cut his hair off, too." [30]

The "discovery" scene is led up to with great skill; Rawdon's arrest is sprung on the reader as on Rawdon himself, and only then does Thackeray wind back over past events to show how Lord Steyne with Becky's connivance had previously got rid of young Rawdon and the "sheepdog" Briggs—"And so two of Rawdon's out-sentinels were in the hands of the enemy." [31] It is as near as he comes to saying that the arrest was framed.

There is a moral comment in the fact that Becky's downfall comes through the relations that she most despised; it is the innocent and stupid who confound her. She calculates brilliantly, but, like Iago, not quite brilliantly enough. Her neglect of her son disturbed Rawdon. When she kissed the child at Queen's Crawley she had not thought that he might say, "You never kiss me at

---

[30] Ch. xiv.

[31] Ch. lii. Greig, missing the subtlety of method, remarks that this chapter "is chronologically misplaced, and was probably an afterthought" (op. cit., p. 116).

home, mother." Lady Jane "never felt quite the same to Becky after that remark." And Lady Jane's simple kindness defeats Becky's calculation, when she releases Rawdon from the spunging-house in time for him to find Lord Steyne at Curzon Street. This is Becky's true nemesis. Contempt for other people is necessary to successful villainy; but within it lie the seeds of its own defeat. The walls of egoism rise, in the end, too high. By suggesting all this, Thackeray does more than condemn Becky; he gives a less pessi-mistic moral direction to his story. Goodness is not wholly in-effectual.

* * *

These, then, are some of the ways in which Thackeray gives shape and purpose to his great pictorial mass; but the most im-portant way has been often undervalued by later readers, because misunderstood. The whole is "brilliantly illuminated by the author's own candles"; Thackeray is constantly present, comment-ing on the action. Only in this novel is it undisguised. Elsewhere he partly identifies himself with a character—Pendennis, or Es-mond; or uses a character as narrator—Pendennis in *The New-comes* and *Philip*, with Clive and Philip as further "projections" within the story. (The latter device, caught, he admitted, from the despised Lytton, was purposeful: "I shall be able to talk more at ease than in my own person.")[32] In *Vanity Fair* there is no disguise; the author is present, with a varying range of visibility. He talks to us, about the story and characters, or about something it reminds him of;[33] he is frankly the manufacturer of the narrative ("there are some terrific chapters coming presently"); he is the "producer" of particular characters (especially of Amelia, who can do so little for herself); he is by turns the responsible, omniscient narrator ("for novelists have the privilege of knowing every-thing"),[34] the irresponsible, baffled spectator ("Was she guilty or not?"), even the mere reporter (himself meeting the characters at Pumpernickel in 1830). Above all he is the moral commentator, the "preacher in cap and bells," amused, melancholy, hortatory—and constantly barbing his shafts with a *de te fabula*. The at-

[32] Letter of August 1853 (*Letters*, III, 298). There is a hint of it in the use of Tom Eaves in *Vanity Fair*, ch. xlvii.

[33] Sometimes with a journalist's sense for the immediately topical, as in ch. lv: "Fifine went off in a cab, as we have known more exalted persons of her nation to do under similar circumstances." This number appeared in April 1848.

[34] Ch. iii.

mosphere of his personality—not his private, but his artistic personality—envelopes the story.

Nowadays, apparently, this practice requires defence; and several lines of defence are valid. There is the historical defence. This method was not new or peculiar to Thackeray, save in extent and subtlety. Behind it lies the tradition of Fielding's role of epic poet, with such modifications as the "comic epic in prose" requires; it is as comedy that Thackeray sees his own novels, and comedy always allows more room for the author. There is also the seeming casualness of Sterne, taking us behind the scenes, showing us the raw material of a novel in process of being worked up. There is also as we have seen the peculiar audience-relation of the serial-writer, reassembling his listeners, responding to their comments with his own. All this helped to make Thackeray's technique easily acceptable in his own time.[35] The average modern reader starts with a prejudice in favour of "dramatic" presentment; the novel having, since Thackeray's time, foregone many of its advantages in favour of a fancied "objectivity," and the novelist having dwindled into invisibility. But to press the historical defence might be to admit a limited appeal: or to suggest that he adopted this method unthinkingly. The true justification lies in its appropriateness to his kind of novel.

Thackeray has often been called the novelist of memory; all his stories are seen retrospectively. "Let us have middle-aged novels," he said in *Rebecca and Rowena*; it is what he gives us, with the light of irony or pathos playing on past fashions and the morning ideals of youth. His commentary is in part a bridge between past and present, suggesting what time changes, what it leaves unchanged; putting past and present alike in a longer perspective. And it is a moral perspective. Thackeray gives us what seems a whole world, densely peopled, varied in scene, with the miscellaneousness and wastage and loose threads of the actual world; but through his comments he makes it plain that he sees the "tower on the toft" above the "field full of folk." The title itself is a comment, the title that came to him in the night "as if a voice had whispered";[36] it suggests both the observer, and the preacher who "cries his sermon." Without Thackeray's own voice, the melancholy and the compassion of his attitude to Vanity Fair might escape us. It is needed merely as relief, from a spectacle

[35] Contemporary objectors were rare; one was G. H. Lewes, in *The Leader* (21 December 1850), p. 929.

[36] *Letters*, I, cxxvi.

that might otherwise be unbearably painful. And not only morally painful, but mentally impoverished. The characters, the best as well as the worst, are almost without ideas; the intellectual atmosphere of the novel is provided by the commentary.

> Can the reader do all this for himself? If he can, and can do it as well as Thackeray does it for him, he may consider it surplusage.[37]

Thackeray does not escape into commentary from any weakness in presentation; *Vanity Fair* is particularly rich in single scenes which reveal his power of presenting characters and action without comment, through dialogue, grouping, and gesture. Nor is he impulsively allowing his stored reflections to overflow; the effect of casualness in the commentary is as calculated as in Sterne. The commentary is itself art, selective and economical. Thackeray never tells everything; he leaves much to be read between the lines; the tone of intimate confidence often masks a real reserve. He knows when not to comment directly at all. Much could have been said on the death of George Osborne; this is all that is said:

> No more fighting was heard at Brussels—the pursuit rolled miles away. The darkness came down on the field and city, and Amelia was praying for George, who was lying on his face, dead, with a bullet through his heart.[38]

It is no simple statement; not only is the immediate reference magnified by the drawing together of Brussels and the battlefield, but its very brevity and the silence surrounding it mark its subject —not the death of one George Osborne, sufficiently shown as odious and contemptible, but Death, sudden, august, and mysterious. But all this is implicit. Yet equally impressive in its own way, and equally enlarged beyond the particular circumstance, is the leisurely commentary on the death of Mr. Sedley;[39] appropriate to a death that is not sudden, but long prepared for, domestic and not dramatic, enmeshed in practical circumstance, and apparently presented as a mere change in habitation. The one method is as essentially part of the novel's texture as the other.

The commentary springs also from Thackeray's wish to "convey

---

[37] Brownell, op. cit., p. 7; and cf. pp. 9–10.
[38] Ch. xxxii, at the close of the ninth number. I do not know how soon Thackeray revised this famous sentence, deleting the opening "The"; certainly by 1853.
[39] Ch. lxi.

the sentiment of reality." Through it he openly admits, as no modern novelist dare, *all* the relations of the novelist to his story. The novelist does write what he knows to be "terrific chapters," he does construct and manipulate his characters, and he is also carried beyond his conscious self ("I have no idea where it all comes from").[40] He remembers, and observes; he is affected, as he writes, by what is happening around him—the "unwritten parts" of novels. Thackeray's candour about all this is part of his love of truth. Believing in truth, he can afford to admit that what he writes is fiction. And the illusion is not thereby broken. When he calls his characters puppets, it is not their smallness, but their separateness from him, that strikes us; and perhaps his own largeness. "Thackeray is a Titan . . . [his words] as solemn as an oracle."[41]

> Ah! *Vanitas Vanitatum!* Which of us is happy in this world? which of us has his desire? or, having it, is satisfied?—Come children, let us shut up the box and the puppets, for our play is played out.

The great picture is not the less great from our final awareness that we and the author stand outside its frame. The words are a recall to life and individual responsibility as the preacher lays his cap and bells aside.

[40] *Letters*, III, 468 n.
[41] Charlotte Brontë, in a letter of 1848. *The Brontes, their Lives, Friendships, and Correspondence*, 4 vols. (Shakespeare Head Bronte, Oxford, 1932), ii, 201.

On the Style of *Vanity Fair*

by G. Armour Craig

. . . there is still a very material difference of opinion as to the real nature and character of the Measure of Value in this country. My first question, therefore, is, what constitutes this Measure of Value? What is the signification of that word "a Pound"?

Speech of Sir Robert Peel on the Bank Charter Acts (6 May 1844)

Perhaps I might be a heroine still, but I shall never be a good woman, I know.

Mrs. Gaskell, *Wives and Daughters* (1866)

"Among all our novelists his style is the purest, as to my ears it is also the most harmonious. Sometimes it is disfigured by a slight touch of affectation, by little conceits which smell of the oil;—but the language is always lucid." The judgment is Anthony Trollope's and the lucidity he praises is Thackeray's: "The reader, without labour, knows what he means, and knows all that he means." [1] The judgment has been shared by many, perhaps even by Thackeray himself, for he was vigilant in detecting "fine writing" or "claptraps" in the work of others,[2] and for himself he insisted that "this person writing strives to tell the truth. If there is not that, there is nothing." [3] Yet some reconciling is necessary, for the truth is not always lucid and lucidity may not always be quite true.

"On the Style of Vanity Fair*" by G. Armour Craig. From* Style in Prose Fiction: English Institute Essays, 1958, *ed. Harold C. Martin (New York: Columbia University Press, 1959), pp. 87–113. Reprinted by permission of the publisher.*

[1] *An Autobiography*, ed. by Frederick Page (London, 1950), p. 244.

[2] See e.g., his review of "A New Spirit Of The Age," *Works—The Oxford Thackeray*, ed. by George Saintsbury (17 vols.; London, 1908), VI, 424; or some advice on "fine writing" in *The Letters and Private Papers of William Makepeace Thackeray*, ed. by Gordon N. Ray (4 vols.; Cambridge, Mass., 1945), II, 192.

[3] Preface to *Pendennis*.

There is at any rate a passage in chapter 42 of *Vanity Fair*[4] for Trollope's judgment of which the modern reader—at least this reader—would give a good deal. It describes the life of Jane Osborne keeping house for her father: her sister is now the fashionable Mrs. Frederick Bullock, her brother, disowned by their father for his marriage to Amelia Sedley, has been killed at Waterloo, and Jane now lives in idle spinsterhood in the great glum house in Russell Square.

> It was an awful existence. She had to get up of black winter's mornings to make breakfast for her scowling old father, who would have turned the whole house out of doors if his tea had not been ready at half-past eight. She remained silent opposite to him, listening to the urn hissing, and sitting in tremor while the parent read his paper, and consumed his accustomed portion of muffins and tea. At half-past nine he rose and went to the City, and she was almost free till dinner-time, to make visitations in the kitchen and to scold the servants: to drive abroad and descend upon the trades-men, who were prodigiously respectful: to leave her cards and her papa's at the great glum respectable houses of their City friends; or to sit alone in the large drawing-room, expecting visitors; and working at a huge piece of worsted by the fire, on the sopha, hard by the great Iphigenia clock, which ticked and tolled with mournful loudness in the dreary room. The great glass over the mantle-piece, faced by the other great console glass at the opposite end of the room, increased and multiplied between them the brown holland bag in which the chandelier hung; until you saw these brown holland bags fading away in endless perspectives, and this apartment of Miss Osborne's seemed the centre of a system of drawing-rooms. When she removed the cordovan leather from the grand piano, and ventured to play a few notes on it, it sounded with a mournful sadness, startling the dismal echoes of the house.   (pp. 441–42)

Thackeray's prose is seldom better than this. The passage comes from a paragraph that comments on the difference between Jane Osborne's life and that of her sister: "One can fancy the pangs" with which Jane regularly read about Mrs. Frederick Bullock in the "Morning Post," particularly the account of her presentation at the Drawing-room. The reader, characteristically, is invited to supply from his own observation the sort of vulgar envy that feeds upon accounts of "Fashionable Reunions" in the newspaper and to look down on Jane Osborne's suffering as no more than the deprivation of the snobbish pleasures of

---

[4] References are to the Modern Library College Editions reprint (New York, 1950), which is based on the edition of 1864.

elegant society. The passage begins, then, easily enough: "It was an awful existence." And "awful" is at first simply a colloquial affectation. It becomes something more, however, as we move in to the account of Jane's routine and ascend from the tremors of the breakfast table to the solitude of the drawing room with its covered chandelier "fading away in endless perspectives": the conversational pitch turns momentarily solemn with the vision of "this apartment of Miss Osborne's" as "the centre of a system of drawing-rooms"—including perhaps even that most august of all such apartments where her sister has been received. It would be hard to find this an example of the "little conceits which smell of the oil," for even here Thackeray does not lose his customary confidential hold upon the reader. The vision is kept close to us by his usual resource: the opposing mirrors "increased and multiplied between them the brown holland bag in which the chandelier hung; until *you* saw these brown holland bags fading away in endless perspectives." The "you" is no doubt as unobtrusive as an idiom. But it is not inconsistent with Thackeray's constant and fluent address to his reader, an address at its best as easy as idiom. In this very short passage Thackeray has moved from an example of the snobbery he loved to detect to a memorable symbol of the society in which snobbery flourishes. It is a society of endless perspectives, a system of drawing rooms whose center is everywhere, whose circumference is nowhere.

But is this what Thackeray meant? And is it the "all" that he meant? Certainly the symbol is not characteristic—it is indeed unique in *Vanity Fair*. Usually, or at any rate perhaps too often, Thackeray renders the barren routines of high life in mock genealogies or in the kind of mildly allegorical guest list that follows this passage. We are told that twice a month the solitary dinners of Mr. and Miss Osborne are shared with "Old Dr. Gulp and his lady from Bloomsbury Square, . . . old Mr. Frowser the attorney, . . . old Colonel Livermore, . . . old Serjeant Toffy, . . . sometimes old Sir Thomas Coffin." *Vanity Fair*, we recall, began as "Pen and Pencil Sketches of English Society," as an extension of *The Book of Snobs*. Yet Thackeray seems to have felt the need of some larger, more inclusive presiding idea. In the early stages of writing the first few numbers he "ransacked" his brain for another title, and "Vanity Fair," he said, came to him suddenly in the middle of the night.[5] It seems to have summed up for him a

[5] Gordon N. Ray, *Thackeray: The Uses of Adversity: 1811–1846* (New York, 1955), pp. 384–85.

position from which he could confidently go on with his "Novel without a Hero," but a position of course very different from John Bunyan's. The original Vanity Fair as described by Evangelist is the dwelling place of abominations. But it is after all only one more obstacle on the road to the Celestial City, and all such obstacles are rewards in disguise. "He that shall die there," says Evangelist, "although his death will be unnatural, and his pain perhaps great, he will yet have the better of his fellow." While there are some unnatural and painful deaths in Thackeray's Fair, there seems to be no act of resistance or sacrifice by which anyone can get the better of anyone else, and the irony of the title has no doubt been lively in the minds of many readers. But Evangelist lays down a more poignantly ironical prescription: "he that will go to the [Celestial] City, and yet not go through this Town [where Vanity Fair is kept], *must* needs *go out of the World*." [6] If there is no Celestial City beyond Thackeray's Fair, and if there is no hero determined to fight on to a heavenly peak, it is even more certain that none of Thackeray's characters shall go out of this world. On every page of *Vanity Fair* we find description, exposure, comment, from a position much less elevated and secure than that of an evangelist, yet one from which we do see into an "all" as large as a whole society.

Certainly the style of all this commenting and exposing is this-worldly to a degree that would have puzzled Bunyan as much as it has troubled some of his descendants. In the preface to *Pendennis* Thackeray speaks of his work as "a sort of confidential talk between reader and writer," and it was the excess of this conception of himself—"the little earmark by which he is most conspicuous"—that Trollope found "his most besetting sin in style." The "sin" is "a certain affected familiarity": Thackeray "indulges too frequently in little confidences with individual readers, in which pretended allusions to himself are frequent. 'What would you do? what would you say now, if you were in such a position?' he asks." [7] Yet for Trollope, although this familiarity might breed occasional contempt, it did not finally compromise the great virtue of Thackeray's lucidity. "As I have said before, the reader always understands his words without an effort, and receives all that the author has to give." [8] But to know what, and

[6] *The Pilgrim's Progress* . . . , ed. by Edmund Venables, rev. by Mabel Peacock (Oxford, 1925), pp. 82 ff.

[7] Anthony Trollope, *Thackeray* (London, 1879), pp. 197–98.

[8] *Ibid.*, p. 198.

to know all, a writer means is to be in his confidence indeed, and it would be a serious lapse of style that this confidence should break down in affectation or something worse.

In "Before the Curtain," the preface he wrote in 1848 for the completed novel, Thackeray promises his reader "no other moral than this tag to the present story," that after wandering with him through the Fair, "When you come home, you sit down, in a sober, contemplative, not uncharitable frame of mind, and apply yourself to your books or your business." He raises no literary expectations, he promises no carefully graduated feast of human nature, he does not even excuse himself to those who find all Fairs "immoral" and hence refuse to enter this one. The stern moralists may be quite right in withholding their custom, but those "of a lazy, or a benevolent, or a sarcastic mood, may perhaps like to step in for half an hour and look at the performance." This casualness, the queer juxtaposition of "lazy," "benevolent," and "sarcastic," may seem like the very height of good breeding. It does sum up the uncomfortable collocation of responses that any reader must make to some stretches of the novel. But it also promises that this writer will keep us free from violent emotions as we read. It is the guarantee of a special detachment.

Such detachment is often suggested by a coy version of one of Fielding's comic devices. When we witness the departure of Becky and Amelia from Chiswick Mall, the last flurry of farewells is recounted thus: "Then came the struggle and the parting below. Words refuse to tell it. . . ." The congregation of servants and pupils, the hugging and kissing and crying are such "as no pen can depict, and as the tender heart would fain pass over" (chap. 1, p. 6). Or, on the morning after the fatal excursion to Vauxhall, Joseph Sedley lies "groaning in agonies which the pen refuses to describe" (chap. 6, p. 55) while he suffers the aftermath of rack punch. Becky, disappointed in her attempt to capture Joseph, goes away from the Sedley house to her duties as governess: "Finally came the parting with Amelia, over which I intend to throw a veil" (chap. 6, p. 61). Such mild affectations as these amuse a good deal less than their frequency suggests they should, however obliquely they may glance at sentimental explorations of young female affection or the tract-writer's interest in the heavy repentance of the drunkard. But they are the simplest and the least interesting form of a larger kind of detachment.

About other episodes the narrator is more artfully silent. Perhaps the most interesting is the courtship of Rawdon Crawley, which extends over several chapters and is concealed in the narrative of Becky's ministrations to old Miss Crawley. It will be recalled that the success of Becky's attentions to this lady, the old aunt whose wealth is the object of all the Crawleys' envy and scheming, alarm Mrs. Bute Crawley—whose portrait, incidentally, as well as that of her family and of her husband the Rector, make one wonder that Thackeray could have quarreled with Jerrold's anticlericalism.[9] Mrs. Bute's scheming to secure Miss Crawley's money for her own leads her to warn Rawdon that when his stepmother dies, old Sir Pitt will marry Becky. Rawdon's response sets the level of intrigue exactly:

> "By Jove, it's too bad," thought Rawdon, "too bad, by Jove! I do believe the woman wants the poor girl to be ruined, in order that she shouldn't come into the family as Lady Crawley."
>
> (chap. 14, p. 133)

He proceeds to the recommended seduction, but is outguessed by the frank and outraged role that Becky adopts when he "rallie[s] her in his graceful way about his father's attachment." The game goes on, Miss Crawley recovers from her surfeit under Becky's assiduous care, and shortly news comes that the meek Lady Crawley is dead. Rawdon and his aunt discuss the matter while Becky stands by.

> Rebecca said nothing. She seemed by far the gravest and most impressed of the family. She left the room before Rawdon went away that day; but they met by chance below, as he was going away after taking leave, and had a parley together.   (chap. 14, p. 143)

And the next thing we know, old Sir Pitt has come to town and is down on his knees to ask for the hand of Becky. The narrator comments:

> In the course of this history we have never seen her lose her presence of mind; but she did now, and wept some of the most genuine tears that ever fell from her eyes.   (chap. 14, p. 144)

But what does "genuine" mean here? Or "they met by chance" in the passage above? Are we to infer that during their "parley" Becky uses the threat of a proposal from the father to make sure of the son? Are we to infer that the tears are genuine because she has planned too well—the threat she has used to get

---

[9] See Ray, *Uses of Adversity*, pp. 370–71.

one husband has turned out to be prophetic, and she might have had the father? Are they tears of rage? of regret? As we move on to the next chapter we certainly find no circumstantial report of when and how Becky and Rawdon are married; instead there is a good deal of indirect veiling of the scene and refusing of the pen. "How they were married is not of the slightest consequence to anybody." Perhaps, it is conjectured, they went off one afternoon when Becky was presumed to be visiting Amelia. But the matter is left in uncertainty. On the one hand, "Who needs to be told, that if a woman has a will, she will assuredly find a way?" And on the other: "who on earth, after the daily experience we have, can question the probability of a gentleman marrying anybody?" (chap. 16, p. 153).

The concealment of the circumstances of the marriage may appeal to the lazy, may satisfy the benevolent, and it may give the sarcastic something to work on too. But its most important effect is that the narration here, clustered about with confidential comments and dismissive questions, sets before us a way of knowing the world. It is a way so inferential, so dependent upon unfinished implications, that it comes close to the character of gossip. And a good gossip, while its unfinished sentences and its discreet and indiscreet omissions may keep us from the exhilaration of indignation or rhapsody, can suggest values and insights superior to the vocabulary of the purveyor or the listener. Here, whatever the meaning of that "by chance" that modifies the meeting of Becky and Rawdon, or whatever the meaning of that "genuine" that modifies her tears, we can only infer that the marriage is the result neither of grand passion nor of mean seduction. The veiling of the secret here means that we can only accept Becky's marriage as a convenience. Even the grossness of Mrs. Bute's plotting is lost in the shadows.

The questions with which Thackeray disposes of this affair— "Who needs to be told . . . who can question the probability . . ."—are of course the most conspicuous earmark of his detachment in *Vanity Fair*. There is the issue of who made the first move in Becky's first romance, with the young Reverend Mr. Crisp who came infatuated to tea at Chiswick Mall: after a parenthetical cloud of hints and counter-hints the narrator concludes, "But who can tell you the real truth of the matter?" (chap. 2, p. 14). Just as when the pen refuses to tell, the implication here is only coy. But a good many hundred pages later, in what is called "A Vagabond Chapter" (chap. 64), this kind of coyness can exasperate.

It comes in a passage summarizing Becky's career after her fall from polite society in London: "When she got her money she gambled; when she had gambled it she was put to shifts to live; who knows how or by what means she succeeded? . . . The present historian can give no certain details regarding the event" (p. 681). The detachment inculcated here is vast and affluent indeed; it is perhaps matched only by the elaborate veiling of the circumstances of Joseph Sedley's death. But the most puzzling questions in the book are those that comment upon its crucial passage.

Every reader of *Vanity Fair* remembers the "discovery scene" of chapter 53—the scene in which Becky suffers exposure and isolation after her husband and Lord Steyne violently clash. And every student of the novel knows that this scene is a battleground upon which the judgments of a number of Thackeray's critics have collided. Rawdon, having been freed from the spunging house, hurries "across the streets and the great squares of Vanity Fair, and bursts in upon his wife and Lord Steyne in something less than *flagrante delicto* though ready for embarrassment."

> Steyne was hanging over the sofa on which Becky sate. The wretched woman was in a brilliant full toilette, her arms and all her fingers sparkling with bracelets and rings; and the brilliants on her breast which Steyne had given her. He had her hand in his, and was bowing over it to kiss it, when Becky started up with a faint scream as she caught sight of Rawdon's white face. At the next instant she tried a smile, a horrid smile, as if to welcome her husband; and Steyne rose up, grinding his teeth, pale, and with fury in his looks.
>
> He, too, attempted a laugh—and come forward holding out his hand. "What, come back! How d'ye do, Crawley?" he said, the nerves of his mouth twitching as he tried to grin at the intruder.
>
> There was that in Rawdon's face which caused Becky to fling herself before him. "I am innocent, Rawdon," she said; "before God, I am innocent." She clung hold of his coat, of his hands; her own were all covered with serpents, and rings, and baubles.
>
> "I am innocent.—Say I am innocent," she said to Lord Steyne.
>
> He thought a trap had been laid for him, and was as furious with the wife as with the husband. "You innocent! Damn you!" he screamed out. "You innocent! Why, every trinket you have on your body is paid for by me. I have given you thousands of pounds which this fellow has spent, and for which he has sold you. Innocent, by—! You're as innocent as your mother, the ballet-girl, and your husband the bully. Don't think to frighten me as you have done others. Make way, sir, and let me pass"; and Lord Steyne seized

up his hat, and, with flame in his eyes, and looking his enemy
fiercely in the face, marched upon him, never for a moment doubt-
ing that the other would give way.

But Rawdon Crawley springing out, seized him by the neckcloth,
until Steyne, almost strangled, writhed, and bent under his arm.
"You lie, you dog!" said Rawdon. "You lie, you coward and villain!"
And he struck the Peer twice over the face with his open hand,
and flung him bleeding to the ground. It was all done before Rebecca
could interpose. She stood there trembling before him. She admired
her husband, strong, brave, and victorious.

"Come here," he said.—She came up at once.

"Take off those things."—She began, trembling, pulling the jewels
from her arms, and the rings from her shaking fingers, and held
them all in a heap, quivering, and looking up at him. "Throw them
down," he said, and she dropped them. He tore the diamond
ornament out of her breast, and flung it at Lord Steyne. It cut him
on his bald forehead. Steyne wore the scar to his dying day.

(PP. 554–55)

The theatricality of the passage—Becky's clinging and quivering, the serpents and baubles on her hands, Rawdon's springing
out and his terse manifesto, the flame in the eyes of the wicked
nobleman and the lifelong scar on his head—all such features
suggest that the creator of Punch's Prize novelists is once again
engaged in something like parody.[10] On the other hand it has
been asserted that far from a joke, the scene "is the chief ganglion
of the tale; and the discharge of energy from Rawdon's fist [*sic*]
is the reward and consolation of the reader." [11] The most extensive criticism of the scene finds it unprepared for and conveyed by a dramatic technique foreign to Thackeray's genius,[12]
but this judgment has in turn been disposed of by another critic
who finds Thackeray's usual stamp upon it and some other
felicities as well. He suggests that one of these is the way in which
"Steyne wore the scar" echoes "Steyne wore the star." [13] By the
same sort of reasoning we might infer from "He tore the diamond

[10] As has been suggested by Kathleen Tillotson, *Novels of the Eighteen-Forties*
(Oxford, 1954), pp. 233–34.

[11] Robert Louis Stevenson, "A Gossip on Romance," *Memories and Portraits*
(New York, 1910), p. 239 (Vol. 17 of the Biographical Edition of the *Works*).
Stevenson's judgment is endorsed by Professor Ray in *Uses of Adversity*, p. 410.

[12] Percy Lubbock, *The Craft of Fiction* (London, 1954), pp. 101 ff. Lubbock's
argument has been criticized by Professor Ray (*Uses of Adversity*, pp. 409–10)
and by Geoffrey Tillotson, *Thackeray the Novelist* (Cambridge, 1954), pp. 82 ff.

[13] G. Tillotson, *Thackeray the Novelist*, p. 84.

ornament out of her breast" that Becky's heart is surpassing hard; and certainly Thackeray tells us that the battle takes the heart out of her. But the one touch upon which Thackeray himself is known to have commented is Becky's response to the sudden burst of energy from Rawdon: "She stood there trembling before him. She admired her husband, strong, brave, and victorious." Of this observation Thackeray is reported to have said that it was a touch of genius,[14] and it does consort well with his special genius in the rest of the book.

For although the battle seems to be the expression of outraged honor, it is a collision that misses its main issue and prize. As the resistless masses meet, Becky stands off to one side, and although her admiration is unacceptable or even unknown to Rawdon, and although we are told that her life seems so "miserable, lonely, and profitless" after Rawdon has silently departed that she even thinks of suicide, there is still a profound irrelevance in this violent scene. Becky's maid comes upon her in her dejection and asks the question that is in every reader's mind: *"Mon Dieu, madame, what has happened?"* And the "person writing" concludes this crucial chapter with an enlargement of the same question:

> What *had* happened? Was she guilty or not? She said not; but who could tell what was truth which came from those lips; or if that corrupt heart was in this case pure? All her lies and her schemes, all her selfishness and her wiles, all her wit and her genius had come to this bankruptcy.   (p. 556)

Becky lies down, the maid goes to the drawing room to gather up the pile of trinkets, and the chapter ends. If Thackeray has not risen to a cruel joke on those readers who find consolation and reward in the discharge of energy from Rawdon, he has at least interrupted their satisfaction.

Lord Steyne's meaning of "guilty"—"He thought a trap had been laid for him" by Becky and Rawdon—is of course quite false, though it corroborates the characterization of Steyne as one experienced in double-dealing. "Guilty" from Rawdon's point of view of course means, as he tells Pitt next day, that "it was a regular plan between that scoundrel and her" to get him out of the way (chap. 54, p. 559). And Thackeray goes to as great lengths to make it impossible for us to know that this interpretation is true as he does to conceal the timing and motives of Becky's

---

[14] See Ray, *Uses of Adversity*, p. 500, n. 19; and *Letters and Private Papers*, II, 352[n].

marriage. To see the entangling and displacing of any clear answer, we need only ask "guilty of what?" The usual answer is of
course "guilty of adultery" (or guilty of getting ready for it),[15]
and Thackeray's silence is commonly attributed to his awareness
of the "squeamishness" of his public. Indeed he himself lends real
authority to this account of the matter. In 1840, writing on Fielding, he complains that the world no longer tolerates real satire.
"The same vice exists now, only we don't speak about it; the
same things are done, but we don't call them by their names." [16]
And in *Vanity Fair* he complains that he must be silent about
some events in Becky's later career because he must satisfy "the moral
world, that has, perhaps, no particular objection to vice, but an
insuperable repugnance to hearing vice called by its proper
name" (chap. 64, p. 671). There may well be evidence in Thackeray's personal history to suggest in addition that he was, perhaps
even before the separation from his mad wife, evasive and unclear
on the subject of sexual behavior. But however complicated the
tensions of Thackeray's own emotional experience, and however
rigid the scruples of his audience, the answer to the questions
with which he comments on this most important episode cannot
be a single "name" or possess any "proper name." For he has led
us here, however uneasily, with mingled attitudes of parody and
outrage, to a startling though incomplete vision of a new social
world, a vision exactly proportioned to the irrelevance of the
violence we have witnessed.

The words of the passage that command our moral response
are precisely those that most nearly approach parody: Becky
responds to a nameless "that" in Rawdon's face by exclaiming
"I am innocent." If the reader trained in melodrama scoffs at
the response and turns Becky into a consummate villain, he will
have some trouble getting through the rest of the novel, and it
is likely that he will long since have become exasperated with
Thackeray's tone, his silences and implications. The same is true,
moreover, of the sentimental reader who throws down the volume
and declares that Becky has been monstrously wronged and victimized by wicked men in a bad world. But the reader who says,
in effect, "it is impossible to tell whether or of what she is guilty"
is exactly in the difficult position of one who accepts Thackeray's
narrative as it is given. And what such a reader sees from this
position must fill him with wonder if not dismay. For he sees that

[15] See, e.g., Ray, *Uses of Adversity*, p. 502, n. 14.
[16] *Works*, III, 385.

while he wants to answer these questions, he cannot do so, and he can only conclude that he is looking at a situation before which his moral vocabulary is irrelevant. Becky in her isolation has finally gone out of this world, and it will take a new casuistry to bring her back. Thackeray uses some strong moral words in his comment, it is true: "who could tell what was truth which came from those lips; or if that corrupt heart was in this case pure?" But while we know that Becky has lied heartily to Steyne, and to his hearty admiration, we cannot know that she is lying to Rawdon when she insists on her innocence. Whatever corruption we may have seen, the question this time is in earnest. The qualities named in the final statement, and especially by its last word, tell us where we are: "All her lies and her schemes, all her selfishness and her wiles, all her wit and her genius had come to this bankruptcy." For these are the terms not so much of moral as of financial enterprise, and "this bankruptcy" is the real touch of genius in the passage. Thackeray's questions and his comment express neither indignation nor sympathy. Rather, they bring before us the terrible irresolution of a society in which market values and moral values are discontinuous and separate. And Thackeray will not—he can not—support us as we revolt from such a spectacle.

The ghostly paradigm upon which human nature plays in *Vanity Fair* is the credit economy that in Thackeray's own lifetime finally developed from a money economy. Even the constant gambling in Thackeray's Fair, historically appropriate as it may be to his Regency setting (and much of his own early experience as it may reflect), suggests the unpredictability of the system. Distant though the gambler may be from respectability, his luck is only a little less mysterious than the power his winnings confer upon him. However it may be in the most famous conversation recorded in modern literary history, it is all too true in *Vanity Fair* that rich people are different because they have more money. Thackeray exposed himself to some high-minded criticism from George Henry Lewes when he published the number containing Becky's famous reflection, "I think I could be a good woman if I had five thousand a year." For he had commented, "And who knows but Rebecca was right in her speculations—and that it was only a question of money and fortune which made the difference between her and an honest woman?" (chap. 41, p. 436). In its interrogative form the comment is much more precise than the declaration Thackeray wrote to Lewes. The latter called it "detestable" to say that "honesty is only the virtue of abundance." Thackeray replied that he meant "only that he in the possession of luxuries . . . should be very chary of despising poor Lazarus on foot, and look very humbly and leniently upon the faults of his less fortunate brethren." This is of course no answer; or if it is, it asks for a curious forbearance towards Becky Sharp. But Thackeray qualifies at once: "I am quite aware of the dismal roguery . . . [which] goes all through the Vanity Fair story—and God forbid that the world should be like it altogether: though I fear it is more like it than we like to own." [17] The likeness to "the world" is in the belief that money is magic and in the frightening awareness, no doubt recently reinforced by the financial crisis of 1847, that no theory had yet been devised to control it. Walter Bagehot, in the *Economic Studies* he was composing in the 1870s, confessed to "a haze" in the language in which he described the growth of capital, and he remarked too with admiration that "a very great many of the strongest heads in England spend their minds on little else than on thinking whether other people will pay their debts." [18] For him that system was "marvellous" by which "an endless succession of slips of written promises should be turned into money as readily as if they were precious stones"—so marvelous indeed that it "would have seemed incredible in commerce till very recent times." [19] Thackeray's attitude, doubtless shaped by the short period he spent as a bill broker in 1833—an episode he apparently tried hard to forget [20]—was not so admiring. His Fair, at any rate, is a market the movements of which are perplexing in the extreme.

The first mention of the "guilt" or "innocence" of Becky's relations to Lord Steyne comes in a passage about the "awful kitchen inquisition" of the servants of Vanity Fair. We are told that Raggles, the retired butler of Miss Crawley, who owns the house in Curzon Street where Becky and Rawdon live well on nothing a year, is ruined by his extension of credit to them. But he is the victim of something more than the simple excess of liabilities over assets. The *"Vehmgericht* of the servants'-hall" early pronounces Becky guilty:

> And I shame to say, she would not have got credit had they not believed her to be guilty. It was the sight of the Marquis of Steyne's carriage-lamps at her door, contemplated by Raggles, burning in the

---

[17] *Letters and Private Papers,* II, 353–54.
[18] *The Works and Life of Walter Bagehot,* ed. by Mrs. Russell Barrington (10 vols.; London, 1915), VII, 248, 131.
[19] *Ibid.,* p. 251.
[20] See *Uses of Adversity,* pp. 159–60.

blackness of midnight, "that kep him up," as he afterwards said; that, even more than Rebecca's arts and coaxings.

(chap. 44, pp. 461–62)

The question of guilt here is quite subordinate to the question of credit, and Raggles is ruined not because he is right about Becky's guilt but because he believes in a strict correlation between Becky's moral and financial status. The last of Raggles is seen at the drunken party of the servants on the morning after the battle; our last glimpse of him is not as he suffers in ruin but as he looks at his fellows "with a wild surprise" upon hearing from Becky that Rawdon "has got a good appointment" (chap. 55, p. 565). It is no wonder that Thackeray should have said in a letter to his mother written during the very month when the "discovery scene" appeared,

> I cant find the end of the question between property and labour. We want something almost equal to a Divine Person to settle it. I mean if there is ever to be an elucidation of the mystery it is to be solved by a preacher of such novelty and authority, as will awaken and convince mankind—but O how and when? [21]

Whatever the fate of the larger question, Thackeray does do some novel preaching upon bankruptcy in one section of *Vanity Fair*. John Sedley, we recall, is ruined in the uncertainties following Napoleon's escape from Elba (chap. 18, pp. 170 ff.), and Thackeray's extended portrait of the "business and bustle and mystery of a ruined man" (chap. 20, p. 195) seems at first sight disproportionate. Of course the bankruptcy accounts for the career of Amelia, but not for all of it. For old Osborne, who also emerges from the background just here, is described as behaving towards his former friend Sedley "with savageness and scorn." Our attitude is shaped precisely by Osborne's insisting that as a bankrupt Sedley must be wicked—that he is both out of business and out of the circle of decency. "From a mere sense of consistency, a persecutor is bound to show that the fallen man is a villain—otherwise he, the persecutor, is a wretch himself" (chap. 18, p. 173). And Osborne is characterized more grossly still by his opposition to Amelia for his son, by his insistence that George marry the rich mulatto Miss Swartz, and by his vast self-righteousness. Osborne is perhaps an inept caricature of the City man who has succumbed completely to the superstitions of money, but he is a new kind of portrait, and one not less complicated than Dickens's portrait of another hard

[21] *Letters and Private Papers*, II, 356.

businessman whose adventures were being issued in installments at the same time.

While Thackeray's Mr. Osborne is a crude warning to those who identify bankruptcy and corruption, Dickens's Mr. Dombey is an astonishing testimonial to the degree of violence that must be exerted to link the experience of bankruptcy with moral reform. In the same month, March of 1848,[22] in which they read of the collision between Rawdon and Lord Steyne, readers who followed both authors were shaken by a passage of dreadful violence that describes a collision between Mr. Dombey's manager, Carker, and a railway engine (chap. 55). Dombey witnesses the event and faints at the sight—it is not an "accident" but the physical embodiment of a terrible obsession. When we next encounter Dombey (chap. 58) he is superintending the bankruptcy of his firm which results from Carker's secret machinations and which he will do nothing to avert. He is alone in the world, for he has driven away his gentle daughter Florence, and he is a "ruined man." With gruesome immediacy he thinks of suicide, but just before the knife strikes, his daughter rushes in, a great reconciliation and redemption occurs, and Mr. Dombey, no longer worth five thousand or very much of anything a year, is at last a good man. For all his inventive energy Dickens cannot make clear the relation between the departure of Carker from this world and the moral conversion that Mr. Dombey then undergoes. But this number of *Dombey and Son* together with the contemporaneous number of *Vanity Fair* suggests the extreme lengths to which two of the most sensitive minds of the mid-century were driven in their effort to reconcile the mysterious power of finance capitalism with the requirements of private morality. "Sell yourself" still meant the worst degradation, but the time was approaching when it would become a formula for "success."

In *Vanity Fair* at any rate Becky's bankruptcy offers no clearer connection between villainy—or goodness—and loss of credit than does the situation of Old John Sedley that Osborne so ruthlessly categorizes. The thoroughness with which Thackeray has covered his tracks suggests that no single transaction, not even payment by adultery, is at issue here. The kind of credit upon which the Crawleys lived so well in London and Paris is beyond the power of any act or value to overtake, for it is the social version of that system in which the perpetual promise to pay is taken for the perpetual

[22] See K. Tillotson, *Novels of the Eighteen-Forties*, p. 318.

fact of payment. "The truth is, when we say of a gentleman that he lives well on nothing a year, we use the word 'nothing' to signify something unknown" (chap. 36, p. 374). It may be that Rawdon and Becky are "wicked," but their wickedness will not account for their credit as they pursue the fashionable life. Just as the war that so mysteriously yet inevitably ruined John Sedley was, as Thackeray tells us, a lucky accident interrupting the endless double- and triple-dealing among nations (chap. 28, pp. 279–80), so for Becky an accident interrupts the double-dealing and counter double-dealing of the scramble for social power. The perspectives here are indeed almost endless; they are certainly beyond the limits of innocence or guilt. Even Rawdon, who experiences something like conversion or reform as Becky's career reaches its height, is not quite secure. His one assertion to Becky after the battle is an ironic fulfillment of Steyne's accusation: "You might have spared me a hundred pounds, Becky, out of all this—I have always shared with you" (chap. 53, p. 556).[23] And the last words he speaks in the novel are as ambiguous as any question from the narrator:

> "She has kep money concealed from me these ten years," he said. "She swore, last night only, she had none from Steyne. She knew it was all up, directly I found it. If she's not guilty, Pitt, she's as bad as guilty, and I'll never see her again, never." (chap. 55, p. 579)

It is hardly possible to find the outrage of manly honor in these exactly struck last words. The distinction between "guilty" and "as bad as guilty" would be the final viciousness if it were not the final irrelevance.

But, again, is this what Thackeray means, and is it the *all* that he means? We can believe so only by acknowledging that the easy confidence between reader and writer promised at the beginning has been renounced, for we are here outside the domain of laziness, benevolence, or sarcasm. If the renunciation were the deliberate act of a supreme ironist who turns and rends us for our naive acceptance of his confidential detachment, Thackeray would indeed have created a masterpiece. But in the crucial scene and in portions of the chapters that lead to it Thackeray has exposed us to violent emotions that no politeness can conceal. The enmity between Little Rawdy and Lord Steyne, for example, is an extension of Becky's neglect of her child that erupts into physical violence: Becky boxes his ears for listening to her on the stairs as

---

[23] For a quite different interpretation, see Tillotson, *Novels of the Eighteen-Forties*, pp. 248, 251.

she entertains Lord Steyne (chap. 44, p. 460). The child indeed makes his first speaking appearance in the same chapter as that in which Lord Steyne also first appears, grinning "hideously, his little eyes leering towards Rebecca" (chap. 37, p. 389). The juxtaposition is emphasized when little Rawdon is apostrophized:

> O thou poor lonely little benighted boy! Mother is the name for God in the lips and hearts of little children; and here was one who was worshipping a stone. (p. 392)

The appeal is no mere instance of competing with the creator of little Paul Dombey, as everyone who has read Thackeray's letters to his own mother will know. It is an appeal similar to many others in the narrative of Amelia, although there Thackeray is more characteristically reticent. When Amelia and her mother are reunited after her marriage, though Thackeray begins by referring to "How the floodgates were opened," he adds, "Let us respect Amelia and her mamma whispering and whimpering and laughing and crying in the parlour and the twilight." And when Amelia retreats to meditate in "the little room" with its "little white bed" in her old home, Thackeray desists:

> Have we a right to repeat or to overhear her prayers? These, brother, are secrets, and out of the domain of Vanity Fair, in which our story lies. (chap. 26, pp. 262, 264)

Even—especially—if we construe this scene and its secrets as an expression of Amelia's first awareness that she is to be a mother herself, it still involves relationships and sentiments outside the "domain" that Thackeray so thoroughly explored. It is a domain bounded by the "politeness" invoked in that early address to the reader in which the narrator promises "to love and shake by the hand" his "good and kindly" characters, "to laugh confidentially in the reader's sleeve" at the "silly" ones, but "to abuse in the strongest terms that politeness admits of" all those who are "wicked and heartless" (chap. 8, p. 79). Such terms of abuse for the wicked and love for the good are for the most part so polite that we accept them with all the detachment guaranteed by the Manager of the Performance. But the limits of this detachment—its very bankruptcy—can be shown only as we glimpse the howling wilderness outside, where the secrets of private feelings are violently confused with public forces of huge and mysterious dimensions, and where there is neither lucidity nor truth.

What Thackeray does then exhibit within the domain of the Fair is the impossibility of self-knowledge and, in the fullest sense, dramatic change. The most intimate experiences of the self, whether in prayer or in love, in disappointment or in outrage, must be kept outside. Becky's "I am innocent" is no more an articulation of the truth than it is the lucid exposure of a lie. But to put us where we cannot know "What *had* happened" and to face us with the bewildering irrelevance of our polite detachment, Thackeray was driven to an extreme that no style of his could control. He could not be clear without being untruthful, and he could not be truthful without being obscure. He tried to recover himself, it is true, in the subsequent chapters by returning to the conception of Becky that most saves his book. The most interesting feature of her characterization is not that she begins from the ambiguous social position of the orphan and governess— " 'I don't trust them governesses, Pinner,' says the Sedley housekeeper with enormous assurance, 'they're neither one thing nor t'other. They give themselves the hairs and hupstarts of ladies, and their wages is no better than you nor me' " (chap. 6, p. 60). Thackeray is concerned with much more than the favorite Victorian example of social mobility. The greater truth about Becky is that she is a mimic, that she trades on the difference between fantasy and society, between the role and the fact. But the truth of endless mimicry is much too large for the domain of the lucid. It is larger than any drawing room, park, or square of Vanity Fair, and it could be forced in only by an act of violence that darkened lucidity and concealed truth. The casuistry upon which *Vanity Fair* rests is unique, and the responses of many thousands of readers for a hundred years to this much-read book must constitute one of the most erratic subterranean currents of our moral history.

Vanity Fair: An Irony Against Heroes

by A. E. Dyson

Vanity Fair is surely one of the world's most devious novels, devious in its characterisation, its irony, its explicit moralising, its exuberance, its tone. Few novels demand more continuing alertness from the reader, or offer more intellectual and moral stimulation in return. In part, at least, this deviousness can be seen to relate to Thackeray's own life. As Gordon Ray has shown in his admirable biography, Thackeray knew Vanity Fair from the inside, with all the insight of a man engaged in its ways, yet deeply ill at ease. One remembers his complex dissatisfactions with his lot. He regretted his nationality, thinking that he would have written better in some other language—an illusion which his own achievement surely exposes, even if we invoke no other names for the defence. He regretted his century, imagining that he would have been more at home in the eighteenth: but would Swift and Sterne have disgusted him as they sometimes did if this were true? He regretted his occasional poverty, and the restless bohemianism which followed the tragedy of his married life, but this was the very material of his art: without such experiences, he might have remained a clever and savage journalist to the end of his days.

Such dissatisfactions led to the iconoclasm of his earlier days, but they paved the way too for his compassion. He said of himself on one occasion that he was created with "a sense of the ugly, the odd, of the meanly false, of the desperately wicked." The intensity with which he always responded to the human comedy pushed him towards a more radical criticism of society than perhaps he intended. As Walter Bagehot noted, Thackeray acquired a height-

ened sense of human inequalities, of the diversity of criticism to
which the unprotected and poor are especially exposed. One sees
how readily his temperamental restlessness responded to the restlessness of Vanity Fair itself—to its noise and bustle, its surface
gaiety, its instinctive cruelty, its truthlessness and faithlessness, its
occasional courage and resilience, its desolating lack of heart's ease.

Such considerations lead us very naturally towards Thackeray's
pervasive ambivalence of tone. Where does he stand in relationship
to his characters, and to their world? Does he come to them
chiefly as friend or foe? The explicit indications of attitude, which
are numerous enough, and to some readers offensive, do not take
us very far. In the opening pages—beautifully and hauntingly
written, like so much that is to follow them—he presents himself
as a puppet-master, the sole creator of his characters, and their
destiny. By the laws of art, this is self-evidently true: all writers
do invent their characters, and decide what their fate is to be. By
the laws of great art, however, it is a half-truth at best. The greater
the writer, the more likely he is to find other laws taking a hand;
to find as Richardson did in *Clarissa*, and Tolstoy in *Anna Kare-
nina*, that he cannot deal with his own characters as simply as he
may wish. *Vanity Fair* turns out to be a novel where the puppet-
master is, after all, bound by the iron discipline of his own greatness. The characters come alive, and their creator cannot blacken
or praise them superficially without his readers detecting and re-
senting the lie; they come alive in the real world of human morality, where every complexity of sensitive response must be allowed
for, whether the creator fully approves of such complexity or not.
As E. M. Forster has pointed out, Becky Sharp is an outstanding
example of a "round" character; she defies any rule of characterisation that simple logic might prescribe, and becomes as familiar
and unpredictable as if we had known her all our lives. Thackeray,
of course, knew when his characters came alive as well as we do,
and his rôle of puppet-master is only one of the various *personae*
he adopts. Sometimes, he claims the puppet-master's privilege of
knowing his characters' secret thoughts, and telling us what these
are. But at other times he is reticent, as one would be in life; we
are never shown Amelia's deepest moments of grief, though we
know the torment they must be. And very occasionally—though
on particularly important occasions, as it turns out—he throws
open the enigma of life itself as part of his art: who *can* be sure
when Becky is telling the truth?

The reader of *Vanity Fair* soon finds other evidence to belie the notion that artifice and contrivance are all. To an unusual degree we have the sense of a real world going on all round the main characters, full of diversity and colour, full of characters who appear and disappear, enacting at the edge of our consciousness the same patterns of sin and anxiety which hold the centre of the stage. This use of surrounding detail and seeming irrelevance to reinforce the main structure of the book reminds us of Sterne; as, to a lesser extent, does the fluidity of the time-scale that Thackeray adopts. Though there is nothing as obviously eccentric as the digressions and flash-backs of *Tristram Shandy*, we find that Thackeray's narrative does shift backwards and forwards in time in a way not always easy to chart. The effect is of a "real world" into which the novelist's memory dips rather than of an artificial world which he creates as he goes along. Later in the novel, Thackeray represents himself as a man who learns of all the main events by hearsay. The omniscient narrator, the preacher in cap-and-bells, gives way to this further *persona*, middle-aged, curious and detached.

To learn caution about Thackeray's role as puppet-master is to learn caution about the explicit moral judgments of which the novel is full. Some modern critics have blamed Thackeray for saying too much, but this is surely a naive misunderstanding of his technique. The tradition of commenting upon characters goes back at least to Fielding, but even in *Tom Jones* we are kept continuously on the alert. Are we really to admire Master Blifil's honesty as we are told we should, and to look forward to the hanging of Tom at the end? Fielding adopts the pose of a conventional moralist as a challenge, forcing us to match our personal wits and sense of values against his own. In *Vanity Fair* Thackeray pursues a similar strategy, with ironic overtones even subtler in their range. We are reminded of Fielding's influence in the knowing, man-of-the-world asides; in the ferocity, the gusto almost, with which various kinds of hypocrisy are exposed. There is even something of Sterne in Thackeray's willingness to act the fool, to claim the cap-and-bells as his own. But the prevailing tone of *Vanity Fair* is very different from Fielding's, and *a fortiori* from Sterne's. There is a lack of warmth about it in certain moods: if Thackeray had invented Tom Jones he would surely have found his hero more difficult to forgive, whilst Uncle Toby one cannot imagine him inventing at all. For though Thackeray's iconoclasm is in part exuberant, it also has a tinge of bitterness; it is nearer than Fielding and Sterne ever are to despair. Very readily the teasing and flamboyance give way, at moments of strain, to the tone of the preacher, no longer in cap-and-bells, but solemn and prophetic now in his own right. The title of the novel is taken from Bunyan, and though Thackeray has nothing of Bunyan's clear-cut doctrine to depend upon, he shares the occasional mood of a Wisdom writer; religious judgments are inescapably present, though not directly expressed. In the introductory note "Before the Curtain," we are warned of the melancholy induced by Vanity Fair—a melancholy which gives rise to, and shades into, compassion for the suffering and transience of man. Behind the ostensible warmth of tone, which we can never rely on, there is warmth of a deeper and costlier kind. We are involved in the fate of the characters we laugh at, not distanced from them; it really matters to us to know what happens to them in the end.

Obviously Thackeray's tone is a complex affair, where local nuances relate to the strategy of the whole. We are always left wondering what to make of it, whether it really is as simple, or as moderately simple, as it is dressed out to seem. There is the rather arch playfulness, for instance, which surrounds both Becky and Amelia: is this simply a sentimental evasiveness on Thackeray's part, or does it serve some more devious end? On the surface, the archness is tender towards Amelia, sharp (like her name) towards Becky; yet its eventual effect is to diminish Amelia, whilst making Becky appear interesting, and even great. Around Amelia Thackeray deliberately creates a cloying tone, apparently in order to confirm the complacency of his readers, yet really to create in them a growing unease: what *are* these virtues we are being so cosily invited to admire? How *can* we respond with this degree of whimsy to an adult? Around Becky, however, the same tone plays with very different effect. Throughout the novel, she is referred to as "our little schemer," very much as one might speak of a naughty but not wholly unsympathetic child. In the period when her fortunes are at low ebb, and she sinks to being an extremely seedy (though still resilient) adventuress, Thackeray writes about her almost in the tone of *The Rose And The Ring*:

> So our little wanderer went about setting up her tent in various cities of Europe, as restless as Ulysses or Bampfylde Moore Caren. Her taste for disrespectability grew more and more remarkable. She became a perfect Bohemian ere long, herding with people whom it would make your hair stand on end to meet.

The effect of this is so odd that one is tempted to regard such archness here, if not elsewhere, as an aesthetic flaw. The implication is presumably that Becky lived for a time as a courtesan, yet the tone seems designed to deflect attention away from the actual fact. We have only to imagine Shakespeare writing about Cleopatra as a little schemer whose plots would make our hair stand on end to see how far from serious the passage is.

Nevertheless, too much can be made of such blemishes; certainly they exist in the novel, but they should not blind us to the extreme subtlety of the ironic strategy as a whole. I have mentioned the archness of tone at the start because modern readers are especially likely to need guidance on this: they will be alienated by it more immediately than most Victorians would have been, but they may fail to realise that usually, if not always, this is precisely what Thackeray intends. In what follows, I shall assume that he is one of the most sophisticated of our ironists, and that nearly every effect is very exactly and maturely contrived.

* * *

When we look more closely at Thackeray's leading actors, his subtlety soon begins to emerge. Criticism of their personal characters comes very easily to him—too easily, we are immediately forced to suspect. There are Becky's lies and Sir Pitt's meanness, Mr. Osborne's anger and Mrs. Bute's treachery—all very wicked, surely?, as the author takes every opportunity to assert. Such comment is, we sense, a very surface affair; a kind of thin ice, on which we are too effusively invited to skate. Social and religious comments are less explicitly stated, yet they are certainly implied, and with mounting insistence as the full pressure of the novel comes to be felt. It occurs to us, after a time, that these deeper implications may run counter to the simpler personal ones that are paraded on the surface; that things may be very much less simple than they seem. Take, for example, the contrast between Becky and Amelia, around which so much of the action is built. The destinies of the two girls are clearly to be intertwined, the one a conventional heroine (though Thackeray denies her the name), the other a villainess specially designed to make our hair stand on end. As Amelia withdraws from school into her world of money and privilege, Becky is thrown out into the battle of life, with nothing but her wits on her side. We see the girls both trying to catch husbands, the one aided by her mother's socially acceptable stratagems and a good dowry, the other almost fatally handicapped by the lack of these things. At Waterloo we see them with the husbands they have eventually won, Becky triumphant now be-

cause of her inborn resilience, Amelia beginning to sink under
the deeper handicap of her inner nature—her lack of any real
intelligence or talent, or of the courage and will-power needed
when life turns sour. Towards the end of the novel there are
further reversals, and the two girls, both older and sadder, both
soiled by life, neither much wiser, work out the underlying logic
of their lives. Becky has to live now without the husband she has
loved in her way, Amelia has to live with the second husband she
has accepted just slightly too late. During the action the two
women are compared in a great many ways. We see them both as
mothers, Amelia too indulgent, as we would expect, Becky too detached. At times, Becky seems a very false friend to Amelia; she
behaves very badly at Waterloo, and becomes one of the many
people that Amelia has to fear. The actual harm she does is less,
however, than it appears; there is no planned malice in it, since
this is not a sin she has it in her to commit, and George's character
would be the same whatever she did. There is also an evening of
accounts later on: if Becky rather contemptuously harms Amelia
by flirting with her husband before Waterloo, she equally contemptuously does her a good turn as the novel is nearing its end.
This second act—the use of George's old letter to disillusion
Amelia about his memory—is as finely ambivalent as many of the
other decisive actions in the book. At one earlier point, Becky has
reflected that she could crush Amelia by producing George's letter,
but she has had too much casual good-nature to put this to the
test. When she eventually does produce the letter it is in order to
help Amelia, yet her emotions must have included a certain triumph; her motives must have been characteristically mixed.

In the contrast between Becky and Amelia, the moral characters
of the two girls are always involved. At a very deep level, Thackeray was critical of them both. The notion that his attitude to
either can be taken at face value can survive only for a reader of
the most superficial kind. In a letter written to his mother in July
1847 Thackeray had this to say about Amelia (no doubt slightly
over-stating the truth):

> My object is not to make a perfect character or anything like it.
> Don't you see how odious all the people are in the book (with the
> exception of Dobbin)—behind whom there lies a dark moral I
> hope. What I want is to make a set of people living without God
> in the world (only that is a cant phrase) greedy, pompous, mean
> perfectly self-satisfied for the most part and at ease about their su-
> perior virtue.

Just after the novel was finished, he told Robert Bell in another letter:

> I want to leave everybody dissatisfied and unhappy at the end of the story—we ought all to be with our own and all other stories.

Undoubtedly in making these comments Thackeray was sincere, but like all critical comments they are necessarily less subtle than the force of the novel as a whole. For the moment, I should like to concentrate a little on the strategy of characterisation which under-lies such intentions. On the face of it, Amelia is the virtuous girl of the two, sweet and gentle, though with a helplessness that soon begins to cloy. "The charming sweet thing" is a first impression most people have of her, modulating to "the poor sweet thing" fairly soon. At school she has many friends among the girls, but when the battle of life is entered upon nearly all women, includ-ing her mother, come to view her with contempt. To men she remains an object of courteous attention, but hardly an obvious choice (except to Dobbin, who loves her) as a wife. Thackeray himself appears to sympathise with her, and he does in fact estab-lish her tenderness as the virtue it is. But adverse judgments, often rather slyly foisted off on "the world," begin to mount. Her love of George is imperceptive and self-indulgent. She blinds herself to his faults and (more seriously perhaps) refuses to see that he does not love her; duty and dignity are thrown overboard in the pursuit. When she wins George, she has little wit or liveliness to offer in return for the sacrifice which he sees himself as having made. As the novel progresses, her future is increasingly overshadowed by fears, and we sense that she is destined to be a casualty in the battle of life.

Her virtues also turn out to be more tainted than they at first appear. Her great claim to virtue is the passiveness of self-sacri-fice, yet is self-sacrifice, as she practises it, not an insidious self-indulgence in disguise? As a mother she is weakly and harmfully indulgent, as a daughter she fails her parents in their years of need. When George is alive, her love for him is self-willed and self-regarding, when he is dead, the myth of her marriage becomes an evasion of Dobbin's love.

Becky, in contrast, is ostensibly bad, yet her heroic qualities shine out against Amelia's faults. She is sparkling, clever and resil-ient; from her earliest years she has had to live by her wits, and if the world is against her, is this not mainly because she inherited neither status nor wealth? Her anti-social qualities are at least as much the effect of the world's dealings with her as their cause. Thackeray goes out of his way to blacken her character in his opening pages, as though he entirely shares the standards by which she is judged. As she flings Dr. Johnson's "Dixionary" at the feet of good, silly Miss Jemima, we see her convulsed with hatred and rage; when the coach moves off, "the young lady's countenance, which had before worn an almost livid look of hatred, assumed a smile that perhaps was scarcely more agreeable." During her stay with the Sedleys she is accused of envy and covetousness, malice and pride; it seems as though all the deadly sins must be laid at her door. We hear of the time when she was caught "stealing jam" at eight years of age, as if faults which would be venial in a well-to-do child must be accounted mortal in her.

As the action of the novel unfolds, it is true that her sins become more substantial. She wounds Amelia, ruins Raggles, plays fast and loose with a great many friends and admirers, treats her husband (as she does everyone else) with good-natured contempt, though after her fashion she loves him. Her thoughtlessness as a mother is hard to forgive; when Thackeray says "she had no soft maternal heart, this unlucky girl" for once he is not exaggerating the truth. She lives always as a parasite and sometimes, if we take the hints, as a harlot. At the end, it is even suggested that she becomes a murderess—and though this is only malicious gossip and almost certainly untrue, Thackeray's "Who *can* tell?" echoes uncomfortably in our ears.

Despite all this, it is clear that Thackeray overstates the conventional case against Becky knowingly and deliberately, as the case against Tom Jones was overstated by Fielding. When we ask how we come to detect this, and in any way at all to be on Becky's side, the answer takes us nearer to the heart of the book. At one level, it may be simply that Becky's courage and resilience are admirable in themselves, whether they are applied for good or ill; in this familiar sense Thackeray may be of his heroine's party without knowing it, or more likely, knowing it slightly better than he would wish. Another possibility is that our sympathy with Becky is sentimental or indulgent and little more. Some critics, indeed, have written as though this were true of Thackeray himself. His "sentimentality" can be dissociated, they suggest, from his "irony," and regarded as a balance on the other side: when bitter censoriousness has brought Becky down, good-natured sentimentality brings her up again. Tears and laughter alternate like April weather, and the author is simply a creature of his moods. Such a view is, I shall suggest, extremely superficial, but where Becky is concerned there may be a particular reason why it appeals. Criminals always *are* easier to sympathize with from a distance, in literature as in life; Becky is undeniably a character more easy to forgive when she is safely contained in the pages of a book.

None of this, however, does more than scratch the surface of the problem, for surely we do admire Becky, and legitimately, however glad we are to be outside the range of her wiles? The fact is that she *belongs* to Vanity Fair, both as its true reflection, and as its victim; for both of which reasons, she very resoundingly serves it right. Like Jonson's Volpone, she is a fitting scourge for the world which created her—fitting aesthetically, in the way of poetic justice, and fittingly moral, in that much of her evil is effective only against those who share her taint. Dobbin is largely immune to her, since he is neither a trifler, a hypocrite nor a snob. The other characters are all vulnerable in one or other of these ways, and we notice that those who judge her most harshly are frequently the ones who have least earned such a right.

The right to judge is, of course, the crux, for Vanity Fair is a social place, and no critique of individual characters can be conducted in a void. What Thackeray comes near to suggesting, like Bunyan before him, is that a society based upon privilege and money is rotten in some fundamental sense. The very concepts of Christian morality become, in such a context, an evasion; an attempt to visit upon the underprivileged and the unprotected sins which more properly belong to society at large. In a world of class and privilege, the simple ideas of "lying" and "stealing," when applied by the haves to the have-nots will clearly not do. An ideal validity they may have, but in the world as we know it they are turned into a mockery of themselves. How far Thackeray was aware of these implications, or wished to be aware of them, it is hard to say. In the novel, he places both his readers and himself in Vanity Fair. We are all tainted with the Crawley hypocrisy, whether of Mrs. Bute or Miss Crawley, of Sir Pitt or of Becky herself. Exactly here, however (and surely this is intended, too?), a further temptation is put in our way. To be all tarred with the same brush, and to be brought to realise that we are, can be a relief as well as a challenge. Need we really do more than the next man in the way of penance, if we have done no more than he in the way of guilt? To judge ourselves guilty, and read on, is less uncomfortable than setting about a wonderful mending of the world. All satirists suffer from this possible evasion of their challenge, but some perhaps suffer less than others—and a few might be tempted to take the same escape route themselves. In 1848, the year of Revolution as well as the year of *Vanity Fair*, Thackeray confessed himself a Republican but not a Chartist. He had no wish to be associated with the hated "levellers," yet his picture of society is remarkably in tune with theirs. The poison of "snobbery" had always fascinated him, but whereas his earlier satire was boisterous and comic, the satire of *Vanity Fair* reaches more unerringly towards the roots. The Bute Crawleys are supposed to be Christian, but their plots against Rawdon and Becky are evil in a purely competitive sense. Miss Crawley imagines herself to be a liberal and a Republican, but she is as parasitic as Becky herself (they are truly birds of a feather), though at the other end of the moneyed scale. Almost every sin in Vanity Fair can be traced, beyond personal weakness, to the fundamental laws of money and class; to fawn upon the rich and kick the poor is a Christian law of the land. The poison in Vanity Fair infects even the servants. Mrs. Sedley's servants join in the hunt against Becky when she has fallen from grace, her own servants turn against her when Rawdon has stormed off and they sense that her social position is at an end. The poor have more than their chains to lose in Vanity Fair; they have their opportunities for hurting one another as well. If Thackeray went less far than the Marxists in political analysis, it may have been (to give him the benefit of the doubt) because his view of human nature was correspondingly gloomier than theirs.

The whole institution of marriage is bound up with these attitudes, as Thackeray is also concerned to bring home. When Mrs. Sedley is shocked by Becky's stratagems, after her husband has explained them to her, her shock is not to do with prudery but with class. How dare a hired governess of dubious parentage "look up to such a magnificent personage as the collector of Boggly Wollah?" The cruel realism of this becomes still more detestable when it mingles with conscious snobbery and insensitivity—as it does in George Osborne, when he also conspires against Becky's attempts to steer quietly to port in Joseph Sedley's arms. Thackeray's savagery in such passages has been sometimes overlooked, perhaps, by readers who deplore his "prudery" without realising how realistic about sex he can also be. He was reticent about physical love, as all Victorians were, but in *Vanity Fair* there are franknesses that can shock us even now. Becky, for instance, is not a sensual woman at all; given wealth and social position, she would have managed without sexual adventures fairly well. She is willing to marry Joseph Sedley for all his absurdity; and our very revulsion from this, if we experience revulsion, may be only a sentimental lack of realism about marriage of our own. In Vanity Fair, as Thackeray depicts it, sex is as little reverenced or respected as anything else. On the one hand, it is a subject for endless gossip and malice; a common frailty in which we are all likely to be caught out unless we take sufficient care (but if we are caught Heaven help us, since Vanity Fair is understanding but in no way forgiving about those who fall by the way). And on the other hand, it is a powerful asset to a mother looking round for a good catch for her daughter. Though the weaklings of the world like Amelia may think only of love, a mother will think rather of physical attractiveness and charm. These are the true assets she has to trade with in the marriage market—assets almost as substantial as the dowry itself, though who doubts that money speaks a little louder in the end?

In all such matters Thackeray reports faithfully and even ferociously what the world is like, with a directness that speaks very strikingly across a hundred years of sexual emancipation to ourselves. He is willing to show how far from being pure-minded young soldiers are when they joke together, courteous though their attentions to an Amelia may be; he is willing to depict the cynicism of Mr. Osborne, who will readily see George amuse himself with any woman he fancies, as long as he is not mad enough to want to make her his wife. Boys will be boys, says Mr. Osborne in effect, but "unless I see Amelia's ten thousand down, you don't marry her . . . And that's flat." A modern reader is often tempted, I think, to treat this as bitter satire, rather than as the very minimal realism which it is. What Thackeray is saying, surely, is that the flesh has very little chance indeed of triumphing when the time comes for it to do battle with the world.

Our sympathy with Becky, to return to this, is so closely connected with as to be almost inseparable from the context of Thackeray's social realism. Even while conventional judgments are being made against her, a social background is movingly, if less noisily, sketched. We hear of "this dismal precocity of poverty" without surprise. In the contrast with Amelia, it is at once apparent that whereas the one girl is cushioned, the other must fight to survive. Their quest for a husband is similar, but Becky, with no mother to help her, must risk the insults and misunderstandings attendant upon doing everything for herself. And this, really, is why we are on her side: not because we idealise her ruthless

scheming, or foolishly imagine that we should get along rather
well with her ourselves, but because we see the need for what she
does. In a society using Christian values almost wholly perversely,
resilience and energy are forced to know themselves, in a Becky,
as conventional sins. For this reason too we forgive her, for we see
how little right society has to judge her as it does. She is indeed
its reflection, and interesting to us largely because she has the
courage and energy, though so heavily handicapped, to play its
game. We notice that though she employs hypocrisy, she is never
taken in by it herself; she does not make her sin a virtue, and is
to this degree preferable to those who do. She is never revengeful
or consciously hard-hearted; she is able (a really saving grace) to
laugh at herself exactly as though she were someone else.

Reflecting upon this, we see the deeper purposes Thackeray
must have in mind. To a much larger extent than we would
expect, Becky's judgments on people are the novelist's own. When
she writes a letter to Amelia, for instance, mocking the uncouth
and canting inmates of Queen's Crawley, Thackeray assures us
that it is the wicked Becky speaking, and not himself: "Otherwise
you might fancy that it was I who was sneering . . . I who
laughed . . . whereas the laughter comes from one who has no
reverence except for prosperity, and no eye for anything beyond
success." But clearly this dissociation of himself from Becky is
largely false, and the irony is of the two-edged kind we find
throughout. Given that Thackeray himself judges with compassion, and that this quality is one that Becky, by the nature of
things, does not have, the judgments she makes of Queen's Crawley are substantially the same as his own. Because she sees the
standards by which the world actually lives in such sharp contrast
with the standards by which it professes to live, she can judge as
well as exploit it in its chosen terms. For, indeed, she belongs to
Vanity Fair herself, and reform, whether for herself or for it, is
very far from her thought. She glories in the world's game with
all the superior energy and intelligence that she can command. It
may even be fair, if one thinks in these terms, that the comparatively innocent should have to suffer along with the rest. Old
Raggles might seem an innocent victim, but is he not as corrupt
and open to punishment as anyone else? By thrift he assembles his
nestegg, and by trust he loses it; yet his trust is tainted with snobbery, the mark of Vanity Fair is on it for us to see.

The obverse of this is that Becky's character rises in our esteem
as that of her victims sinks. How could her gaiety and courage

have expressed themselves in any more worthy way? Had she been born to position or power, she would have risen nobly to the rôle. " 'It isn't difficult to be a gentleman's wife,' Rebecca thought. 'I think I could be a good woman if I had five thousand a year.' " And so, as the world judges, she could have been. Who would more charmingly distribute charity than a privileged Becky, or more graciously accept in return the world's esteem? She could have been a Queen, we are told, if she had been born to it; and it is apparent enough that she could.

Lacking, however, these natural advantages, Becky knows that the appearance of respectability and wealth must be sought for instead. And since Vanity Fair is as much pleased with the appearance as the reality, until such time as the discrepancy is seen through and the hunt can begin, Becky has all her intuitive understanding of its values on her side. The appearance can be maintained, it is true, only by exceptional effort; the world's homage is bought at a price, and those who cannot pay cash must know how to charm, and flatter, and amuse. For long periods Becky creates and maintains the required appearance; her resourcefulness and gaiety seem never ending, though she knows (as Lord Steyne brutally confirms to her) that she is living in a house built of straw. And she lifts Rawdon up to apparent affluence and comfort with herself. Though others suffer as she does so, and have to suffer, she is a good wife to Rawdon from the first. It is not the least of the novel's ironies that she loses her husband without really deserving to (though the circumstances leading up to this are surrounded with characteristic enigma); and that this last rebuff is the bitterest, the one she needs most courage to survive.

At this point in the novel we surely pity her; and our attitude has by now become a most searching moral comment upon ourselves. Of course we have to judge as well as pity, but have we, as readers, earned the right to judge? Have we even any pity that rings true, or that Becky will need or be prepared to accept if it does? Again and again Thackeray reminds us that we, too, belong to Vanity Fair. To condemn Becky easily is *a fortiori* to condemn ourselves; how are we to make any judgment without resorting to hypocrisies deeper and more shameful than her own? The imaginative power of Thackeray's vision forces the reality of this dilemma upon us; some further dimension must be sought before we can be sure that we have the right. Should it be the religious dimension, perhaps, to which the word "vanity" directs us? Or the political one, to which the whole analysis of class and money appears to point?

As I have already insisted, we can by no means be sure how far Thackeray would have committed himself in such ways. He was no religious mystic, though he catches the profound melancholy of the contemplative; nor was he a political agitator, though the moral of *Vanity Fair* might have seemed obvious to Karl Marx. Most of his explicit comments reinforce the notion that he is criticising human individuals rather than the structure of society as a whole, yet the novel's pattern, I have tried to show, prevents us from leaving the matter comfortably at this.

Perhaps Thackeray never did decide how far the poison at work in Vanity Fair is a social sin, which decisive social action might remove, and how far it is a personal flaw, an ineradicable vanity in the heart of man. The lack of a clear-cut answer may account in part for his restlessness, which we always sense behind the apparently easy elegance of the style. Religious and political solutions can, however, be a form of glibness themselves. Can we expect Thackeray to offer a clearer answer to such problems than we have worked out for ourselves? For at least a hundred years now the western mind has been discovering enigmas and doubts. In extending our understanding and compassion, Thackeray does the work a novelist is chiefly concerned to do.

*   *   *

This brings us to the novel's true greatness, to its claim to be one of the undoubtedly major novels that we have. It was Charlotte Brontë, one of Thackeray's earliest admirers, who said:

> It is "sentiment" in my sense of the term—sentiment jealously hidden, but genuine, which extracts the venom from that formidable Thackeray, and converts what might be corrosive poison into purifying elixir.
> If Thackeray did not cherish in his large heart deep feeling for his kind, he would delight to exterminate: as it is, I believe, he wishes only to reform.

The "deep feeling" and "corrosive poison" are not opposites, but simply different sides of a unified response to life. We sense the capacity for the former in Thackeray's great sonorous phrases about vanity: "Yes, this is Vanity Fair; not a moral place certainly; nor a merry one, though very noisy"; we sense it in the sympathy we are made to feel for nearly all of the characters, even when—

and perhaps especially when—we have also seen them at their
worst. Mr. Osborne's selfishness and tyranny are strongly realised,
yet his suffering when George dies is none the less powerful and
real. Thackeray is able to make us feel pity for a man like ourselves even as we probe the bitter impurities of grief:

> And it is hard to say which pang it was tore the proud father's
> heart more keenly—that his son should have gone out of the reach
> of forgiveness, or that the apology which his own pride expected
> should have escaped him.

Mr. Sedley also becomes, in his ruin, a broken and pathetic figure;
even Miss Crawley comes to an end which we feel to be worse
than she deserves.

The most remarkable example of Thackeray's compassion, however, is surely to be found in his dealings with Amelia. The strategy
of her characterisation is at least as subtle as Becky's, though there
are somewhat different ends in view. In writing of Amelia earlier,
I stressed the main intention of Thackeray's irony: he tries to trap
us into an easy and arch indulgence towards her in order to shatter
this, later, with a very damaging moral critique. But this is half
the story only, and not the half that matters most. It is in keeping
with the subtlety we expect from a major novelist that our disillu-
sionment with Amelia should contain a further trap of its own.
The swing from simple indulgence to simple censure is easy to
make; too easy if morality is to be much more serious than a game.
By shifting the tone of his irony in various puzzling ways, Thackeray invites us not only to see the causes of judgment, but to probe
their validity. With Amelia as with Becky, in fact, we are made
to look beyond conventional judgments to that true situation—
more costly to contemplate—which we so often miss. When Thackeray rebukes our easy sentimentality towards Amelia, he is clearing
the way not for cynicism, but for pity of a truer kind. Cynicism
indeed is not the opposite to sentimentality but its twin, another
kind of shallowness which we too easily swing towards when re-
buked. We discover that though sentimental indulgence is a trav-
esty of compassion, clear-sighted judgment ought to be simply a
stepping-stone on the way. What Thackeray makes us see is that
Amelia is an incurably neurotic woman, destined to unhappiness
whether things go well with her or ill. The contrast between herself and Becky is to some degree a contrast between robust mental
health and mental defeat. Becky survives even the gravest hard-
ships and rebuffs, Amelia remains fearful even when she achieves,

or seems to achieve, her heart's desire. The comments Thackeray makes upon her are always delicately poised. Soon after her marriage—far too soon—we read:

> Her heart tried to persist in asserting that George Osborne was worthy and faithful, though she knew otherwise.

Amelia's "knowledge" is really, of course, a fear: it is the presentiment of evil which always besets her, as a measure, perhaps of her own inadequacy. It is also, however, a justified fear; one senses that she is the kind of person whose fears create situations in which she chooses to live. Her fears are true, in a manner which described as knowledge, moreover, and though paranoia converts fears into "knowledge" in this way, this is not a knowledge by which they are most likely to be fulfilled. Though her fears are only culpable self-deception could fail to see, yet after George's death Amelia suppresses them, building instead a myth of his absolute devotion by which to live. This, in turn, becomes a mode of evasion, both of her responsibilities as a daughter and as a mother, and of the ever-present challenge of Dobbin's love. The suggestions clustering around this situation are typical of Thackeray's complex sense of reality. Even apart from the obvious weakness of Amelia's conduct, its underlying selfishness is relentlessly exposed. She never really considers Dobbin, or anyone else apart from herself—and this despite the fact that self-sacrifice is the virtue always attributed to her, the virtue that she would claim for herself. Further ironies open out from such perceptions. Is Dobbin's fidelity to the living but unresponsive Amelia entirely different from Amelia's fidelity to the dead George? Might not Dobbin's love, unbeknown to Amelia, be the one experience that could have quietened her fears and given her peace?

Our awarness of these cross-currents is beautifully stage-managed; and represents one of Thackeray's most interesting challenges to ourselves. The material for censoriousness is offered in abundance, but is censoriousness the most human response we can make? Not, surely, if we think of life as it is, with all its perversities; with all its intolerable perplexities and burdens, especially for the lonely and weak. Most of the judgments just suggested against Amelia are touched with glibness: true in a sense they may be, but the whole truth is a bigger and more saddening affair. The kind of love Amelia lavishes on George may be excessive, but had he been worthy of it, the situation could have been transformed. If Amelia had had the good luck to fall in love with Dobbin, her particular virtues might have been productive not sour, her lack of intelligence and talent might have mattered scarcely at all. One might blame her, perhaps, for preferring George's good looks to Dobbin's plainness (and indeed if there is a sensualist in the book, Amelia rather than Becky fills the role). But life is like that after all; since we cannot fall in love to order, can Amelia's evasiveness about Dobbin be wholly and honestly blamed? It may also be that certain types of tenderness, of self-sacrifice and reticence, can take root only in such soil as Amelia provides. When Mr. Sedley on his death-bed repents of the harshness he and his wife have shown towards Amelia, he may be recognising a true flaw in their treatment of her (surely he is), and not simply indulging a last nostalgia in the moment of death.

We rush too easily into censoriousness when reading novels, as Thackeray well knew; the luxury of catching fictional characters out in errors can be very readily mistaken for unusual moral maturity in ourselves. Compassion is better than censure, in literature as in life; by involving us as he does with his characters, Thackeray makes this more than usually plain. It is just when we want to judge most harshly that he allows his stress to fall another way—on the perversity of circumstances and the shortness of time, on the need for forgiveness which embraces us all. The most memorable moments in the novel are those when this insight comes to the surface, and the deep currents of feeling crystallise in phrases we are never likely to forget. The tormented striving, the enigma, the restlessness give way to a grander sense of human solitude and need. Things go wrong for this character or that beyond any deserving, and we see him confronting the world bewildered and alone. There is the poignant moment just before Waterloo, when George comes in late to Amelia after his flirtation with Becky, to be with her, as it turns out, for the last time:

> Two fair arms closed tenderly round his neck as he stooped down. "I am awake, George," the poor child said, with a sob fit to break the little heart that nestled so closely by his own.

And there are other moments, no less pure and heartrending, that we remember: Mr. Sedley's confession to his wife of his loss of money, in words as desolating as they are brief:

> "We're ruined, Mary. We've got the world to begin over again, dear."

and little Rawdon Crawley's reaction when the mother whom he once idolised boxes his ears before Lord Steyne:

"It is not because it hurts me," little Rawdon gasped out—"only—
only"—sobs and tears wound up the sentence in a storm. It was
the little boy's heart that was bleeding. "Why mayn't I hear her
singing? Why don't she ever sing to me—as she does to that bald-
headed man with the large teeth?"

We remember, too, Becky's own reflections, characteristically
tough, yet hardly less poignant for that, when during her later
wanderings she thinks again of the husband she has lost:

"If he'd been here" she said, "these cowards would never have
dared to insult me." She thought about "him" with great sadness,
and perhaps longing—about his honest, stupid, constant kindness
and fidelity, his never-ceasing obedience, his good-humour; his
bravery and courage. Very likely she cried, for she was particularly
lively, and had put on a little extra rouge when she came down to
dinner.

To all of us in Vanity Fair, the weak and the strong, the proud and
the humble, the good and the bad, there come such moments,
when after the bustle and gaiety, the hoping and working, the
striving and fearing, we find ourselves downcast and alone. At such
moments, in Thackeray's depiction of them, all the irony and cynicism, the hatred of worldliness and scorn of fools, give way to this
note of a deeper compassion:

Ah! *Vanitas Vanitatum!* which of us is happy in this world? Which
of us has his desire? or, having it, is satisfied?—Come children, let
us shut up the box and the puppets, for our play is played out.

Form, Style, and Content in *Vanity Fair*

by *John Loofbourow*

When in *Vanity Fair* Thackeray fused his early, satiric expressive conventions into an integral narrative form, a new kind of novel was in the making. In earlier fiction, content, form, and style were separate elements; they could be considered individually as subjects in their own right. But in Thackeray's major novels, as in the work of many modern writers, these aspects of fiction are inseparable and the language itself is a creative element. The difference is like the familiar contrast between classic and romantic art.

The classic-romantic antithesis involves a fairly clear distinction between two ways of envisioning the form-style-content relationship—ways that may conveniently be called "illustration" and "expression." In classical or "illustrative" art, it is the writer's subject that is of primary importance; style is only a means of communicating, form a way of organizing, content. The classicist begins by defining his subject; then he selects an appropriate style and plans an effective presentation. In romantic or "expressive" art, the writer's style is part of the content of his work; his words create meaning, and patterns develop in the process—the method is thought of as a continuous act of expression. The antithesis is figurative—in practice no writer can begin without words or continue without a plan. But the disparity implies dissimilar creative methods and the results are as different as Proust from Fielding. So, in the classical, illustrative tradition, Horace's *Ars Poetica* defines style as decorous exposition (*locum teneant sortita decentum*), form as appropriate presentation (*sibi covenientia finge*), and both form and style merely as instruments for conveying rational con-

"Form, Style, and Content in Vanity Fair." *From* Thackeray and the Form of Fiction *by John Loofbourow (Princeton: Princeton University Press, 1964), pp. 73–91. Copyright © 1964 by Princeton University Press. Reprinted by permission of the publisher. The last paragraph is omitted.*

tent (*verbaque provisam rem non invita sequentur*).[1] The proto-romantic Longinus, however, considers the expressive medium to be synonymous with the artistic concept ("the expressiveness of the word is the essence of art").[2]

English fiction before Thackeray was in the illustrative tradition. Eighteenth-century writers—Defoe, Smollett, Fielding— equated the novel's subject with rational content; for these novelists, form was identical with plot, an effective arrangement of the narrative materials; and style was an expository or decorative means of communication rather than a creative medium. If Richardson's structures were less controlled, his style less apposite, it was due to technical insufficiency rather than artistic originality, and Sterne is the exception, as he is to all literary rules. Long after the content of the nineteenth-century novel had become "romantic," the illustrative method continued to control the writing of English fiction; the development of new narrative methods does not date from the break between the early romantic poets and the neoclassical tradition. The technique of the novel remained basically unchanged from Fielding to Thackeray, and a look at some examples will show how far this is true.

Classicism found its superlative exponent in Jane Austen, and *Emma* is its most brilliant example. *Emma's* dramatic form is synonymous with narrative fact and, consequently, with its literal "plot." The novel's climaxes coincide with three objective incidents: an abortive marriage proposal, a misguided flirtation, and a successful marriage. The first is a typical instance. Emma attempts to make a match for her friend, Harriet, and her efforts result in Mr. Elton's indecorous proposal for her own hand—the event is logically prepared, Emma's mistake is defined, and the objective outcome of her actions is the rational penalty for her behavior:

[Preparation] "Depend upon it, Elton will not do . . . he does not mean to throw himself away."

[Analysis] "Nothing so easy as for a young lady to raise her expectations too high. . . . Harriet Smith is a girl who will marry somebody or other."

[Anticipation] "Mr. Elton in love with me!—What an idea!" ". . . I think your manners to him encouraging."

---

[1] Horace, *Ars Poetica*, 11. 92, 119, 311. (Citations to classical texts refer to the Loeb Classical Library edition.)

[2] Longinus, *Peri Hupsos*, 1. 3.

[Event] "It really was so . . . Mr. Elton, the lover of Harriet, was professing himself *her* lover." [3]

The literal event is the precise correlative of dramatic and emotional development, and is sufficient in itself to convey the author's meaning. Emma's willful distortion of reality involves her friend, Harriet, in a self-deception, and the psychological content of the situation is verified by the actor's rational comments: "a very foolish intimacy . . . a very unfortunate one for Harriet. . . . Vanity working on a weak head, produces every sort of mischief." [4] The moral is explicitly drawn, rather than expressively suggested, by Emma herself, who is "resolved to do such things no more": "to take so active a part in bringing any two people together . . . was adventuring too far, assuming too much, making light of what ought to be serious, a trick of what ought to be simple." [5] The delicate precision of these last phrases is the reward of the classical discipline. And every aspect of the novel is equally felicitous. *Emma's* plot is exquisitely correlated with dramatic structure, distinct and iridescent as a Platonic idea: form is an appropriate harmony (*convenientia finge*); moral insights (*rem provisam*) are essential themes. Nowhere does the novel's imaginative content supersede its objective structure or transcend its clear, communicative medium; and this is both an advantage and a limitation.

The melodic consonance of Jane Austen's style is an instance of decorous illustration (*sortita decentum*); and the illustrative technique excludes the expressive diversity of modern narrative prose. Like Parian marble, the classical novel's diction is a common medium, varying only in the degree of rhetorical precision and the effectiveness of the embellishments. The writer's exercise of individuality is confined to the choice of subject and the manner of ornamentation; for all their differences in creative vision and decorative detail, Fielding, Smollett, and Jane Austen write the same fundamental rhetoric. It is impossible, among novelists of this period, to find such stylistic contrasts as between Hardy, Virginia Woolf, James Joyce; and English novelists continued to write illustrative prose until the middle of the nineteenth century.

This proposition may seem untenable when it includes the Brontës, whose fiction seems so distant from the novels of the

[3] Jane Austen, *Emma* (*The Novels of Jane Austen*, Volume IV), ed. R. W. Chapman, The Clarendon Press, Oxford, 1923, pp. 66, 64–65, ch. 8; p. 112, ch. 13; p. 129, ch. 15.

[4] *Ibid.*, p. 64, ch. 8.

[5] *Ibid.*, p. 137, ch. 16.

eighteenth century; but an analysis of their prose makes it clear that they were practicing traditional techniques. Even so "romantic" a writer as Emily Brontë was limited to the common diction. Although the Brontës' visionary effects are not truly compatible with the neoclassical rhetoric that exquisitely illustrated Jane Austen's luminous insights, at the time they wrote, prose narrative had no other language to express dramatic event, and they adapted, rather than altered, the accepted medium. Thus in *Wuthering Heights*, Emily Brontë represents climaxes of pure emotional content by conventional images of physical action that typify but do not express Heathcliff's agony and Catherine's passion: "He dashed his head against the knotted trunk; and, lifting up his eyes, howled, not like a man, but like a savage beast"; "such senseless, wicked rages! There she lay . . . her hair flying over her shoulders . . . the muscles of her neck and arms standing out." [6]

The point is made clearer by comparing Emily Brontë's language with the eighteenth-century diction of Richardson's *Clarissa*, where the same basic rhetoric is used to describe the very different instance of a prostitute's "squalid" death—the "infamous" Mrs. Sinclair's "wickedness" and "rage": "howling, more like a wolf than a human," "her hair" conventionally "torn," "violence" distending "her muscular features." [7] The common rhetoric's neoclassical abstractions—"savagery," "wickedness," "rage"—preclude the expressive representation of complex emotions, which must be conveyed by the author's or actors' rational comments, as they are in Jane Austen; and when the writer attempts to surmount this restriction, the tradition's invariable equation of subjective experience with generalized behavior ("dashed his head," "lifted his eyes") produces an indecorous but persistently formulaic effect.

In *Vanity Fair*, Thackeray writes another kind of prose; he dispenses with rational analysis, but develops a narrative medium whose expressive images convey the novel's emotional event— Amelia at Waterloo, "her large eyes fixed and without light"; Steyne, "with flame in his eyes," defying retribution. [8] In *Wuthering Heights*, similitudes are confined to explicit comparisons— "My love for Linton is like the foliage in the woods . . . my love

---

[6] Emily Brontë, *Wuthering Heights*, The Shakespeare Head Press, Oxford, 1931, p. 192, ch. 16; p. 135, ch. 11.

[7] Samuel Richardson, *Clarissa*, The Shakespeare Head Press, Oxford, 1930, VIII, 56, 57, 55, 66, 67, Letter CXXXVIII.

[8] *The Works of William Makepeace Thackeray* (The Biographical Edition), Harper & Brothers, New York, 1899–1903, I, 284, ch. 30.

for Heathcliff resembles the eternal rocks beneath." [9] In *Vanity Fair*, similes are replaced by metaphors whose suggestive range is amplified by allusion to familiar artistic conventions, as when a sequence of romance motifs culminates in imagery that transforms men to oaks and women to doves: "Oh, thou poor little panting soul! The very finest tree in the whole forest, with the straightest stem, and the strongest arms, and the thickest foliage, wherein you choose to build and coo, may be marked, for what you know, and may be down with a crash ere long." [10]

Thackeray's prose, the crucial factor in his narrative experiment, was an unaccustomed harmony ("Nobody in our day wrote, I should say, with such perfection of style," Carlyle remarked).[11] Among its precursors were the rhythms of Sterne, who brought a conversational flexibility to his narrative style, and the rhetoric of Carlyle, who revived, in prose, the richness of allegorical figuration. Sterne's rhythmic range greatly increased the capacity of the narrative medium to assimilate diverse modes without losing its expressive unity. His stylistic innovation was simple and profound: he put Locke's theory of associated ideas into fictional practice by adapting the informal rhetoric of personal letters or memoirs—cursive punctuations (dots, dashes, parentheses, semicolons, :—, or —!), conversational inflections ("Fy, Mr. Shandy," "O Thomas! Thomas!"), inversions, ellipses, and digressions. There are earlier instances of rhythmic complexity—Swift's "Tale of a Tub," for example—but none in which a story is simultaneously developed. "The machinery of my work," Sterne insisted, "is of a species by itself." Digressions are part of his narration, associations are continuous with statement—"In a word, my work is digressive, and it is progressive too,—and at the same time." [12] It was this freedom of rhythmic movement that permitted Thackeray to integrate diverse expressive textures in *Vanity Fair*—and if the rhythmic resources of Sterne's narrative style enabled Thackeray to assimilate allusive modes, Carlyle's figured rhetoric taught him to fuse these allusions into cumulative metaphor. Carlyle combined the biblical tropes of Donne and Milton with the romanticism of Lamb and De Quincey: "Language is the Flesh-Garment, the Body of Thought,"

[9] Brontë, *Wuthering Heights*, p. 93, ch. 9.

[10] *Works*, I, 111–12, ch. 13.

[11] Quoted by Gordon N. Ray, *Thackeray: The Age of Wisdom*, McGraw-Hill, New York, 1958, p. 420.

[12] Laurence Sterne, *The Life & Opinions of Tristram Shandy, Gentleman*, The Shakespeare Head Press, Oxford, 1926, Vol. I, p. 77, ch. 22, Bk. I.

he intoned in *Sartor*—"Imagination wove this Flesh-Garment," he continued in capitals, "Metaphors are her stuff . . . it is here that Fantasy with her mystic wonderland plays into the small prose domain of Sense, and becomes incorporated therewith." [13]

Sterne and Carlyle are themselves, of course, only particular instances of the complex processes that prefigured the prose of *Vanity Fair*. Sterne's rhythms were imitated by many writers, including the fashionable novelists that Thackeray parodied; Carlyle's metaphors were derived from Goethe and the German romantics, whose work Thackeray knew, as well as from Milton and Donne. But Thackeray's vigorous version of fashionable syncopations is his tribute to *Tristram Shandy*; and *Sartor* is audible in the resonance of his narrative commentary. *Vanity Fair's* diction combines Sterne's punctuations, inflections, and digressive continuities with satirical modifications of Carlyle's symbolism; and this unprecedented synthesis produces characteristic overtones in passages like the classical-biblical parable that shadows forth Rebecca's fate: "the honest newspaper-fellow . . . can't survive the glare of fashion long. It scorches him up, as the presence of Jupiter in full dress wasted that poor imprudent Semele—a giddy moth of a creature who ruined herself by venturing out of her natural atmosphere. Her myth ought to be taken to heart amongst the Tyburnians, the Belgravians,—her story, and perhaps Becky's too. Ah, ladies!—ask the Reverend Mr. Thurifer if Belgravia is not a sounding brass, and Tyburnia a tinkling cymbal." [14]

Vanity Fair, formed on this flexible, allusive prose, is as different from *Emma* and the "classical" novel as Berlioz is from Mozart. Thackeray's characters are refractions of allusive color rather than instruments of rational insight. They do not think. In *Vanity Fair*, thinking is sometimes an emotional response—"She thought of her long past life, and all the dismal incidents of it"—sometimes a subjective conflict—"how she tries to hide from herself the thought which will return to her, that she ought to part with the boy"—sometimes an intuitive judgment—"He loved her no more, he thought, as he had loved her"—but never intellectual analysis.[15] There is no mutual explication, since the characters never communicate rationally: "poor Amelia . . . had no confidante; indeed, she could never have one: as she would not allow to herself the

[13] Thomas Carlyle, *Sartor Resartus*, ed. Charles Frederick Harrold, Odyssey Press, New York, p. 73, Bk. I, ch. II; pp. 219–20, Bk. III, ch. 3.

[14] *Works*, I, 487, ch. 51.

[15] *Ibid.*, p. 520, ch. 53; p. 480, ch. 50; p. 666, ch. 67.

possibility of yielding." These actors represent not intellect deluded but delusion itself. *Emma's* characters often make erroneous choices; in *Vanity Fair*, alternatives are unperceived, and the actors retreat unconsciously from the force of facts: "giving way daily before the enemy with whom she had to battle. One truth after another was marshalling itself silently against her, and keeping its ground." [16] Truth is never confronted in *Vanity Fair;* its inhabitants must be pushed blindfolded over the edge of reality. When Amelia decides at last to relinquish her child, it is in a "burst of anguish": "she was conquered. The sentence was passed." [17] Such characters cannot define or respond to objective event—they hardly recognize it.

The result is that *Vanity Fair's* objective plot-sequence does not control the novel's effective dramatic form. Since the actors respond not to external facts but to inner images represented by allusive motifs and expressive textures, the literal incidents of the novel's "plot" are not correlated with its imaginative events. When Amelia's father loses his fortune, the factual crisis has no effect on dramatic experience. Before the event, distressed by George's negligence, Amelia expects to marry him; after the event, distressed by George's negligence, Amelia marries him. Conversely, when Rawdon dismisses the Marquis of Steyne, Rebecca suffers no literal loss—unlike the social adventuress in *Bleak House*, Lady Dedlock, she has acquired neither wealth nor real prestige; she forfeits nothing but marital security: Rawdon provides her with "a tolerable annuity" [18] and she was always *demi-mondaine*. Again, in the dramatic and central Waterloo episode, literal event is peripheral: malice, jealousy, panic are its subjective phenomena; its only objective incident is dismissed in the last sentence, and is never emotionally or dramatically represented in the narrative context— "Amelia was praying for George, who was lying on his face, dead." [19]

In *Vanity Fair*, factual incident is a convenience for the common reader and the novel's "plot" has no real relationship to dramatic development. Literal event gives no clue to *Vanity Fair's* expressive tensions; thus, the opposition between Becky's and Amelia's fortunes which is felt as a formal principle does not correspond to their objective experiences. A graphic comparison of the heroines' financial and social circumstances, for example, looks like this:

[16] *Ibid.*, p. 481, ch. 50.
[17] *Ibid.*, p. 482, ch. 50.
[18] *Ibid.*, p. 543, ch. 55.
[19] *Ibid.*, p. 311, ch. 32.

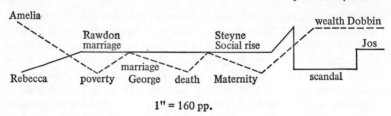

1" = 160 pp.

There is no significant literal relationship between the two fortunes. The heroines' dramatic opposition is not an objective antithesis. Amelia's social status fluctuates erratically, never illustrating the emotional sequence—her prolonged personified journey from amorous confusion to maternal agony. The imaginative pattern of Rebecca's picaresque dramatic progress is not based on financial facts which are statistically monotonous from her marriage to Rawdon through her liaison with Steyne. And Waterloo, since no objective event is represented, has no place in the literal plot, although it is the artistic center of the novel.

Dramatic event in *Vanity Fair* is a very different thing from dramatic event in illustrative novels. Created by the words themselves, the significance of Thackeray's "events" is found in expressive, metaphorical values, not in objective elements. In earlier fiction, narrative incident was an illustration of logical content; *Emma's* final love-scene has no expressive importance: it is an affirmation of rational insights: "She had led her friend astray, and it would be a reproach to her for ever; but her judgment was as strong as her feelings, and as strong as it had ever been before, in reprobating any such alliance for him, as most unequal and degrading. Her way was clear, though not quite smooth." [20] In *Vanity Fair,* there are no rational affirmations to illustrate. The final love-scene draws no morals; instead, its allusive textures assemble, in one expressive realization, the successive satiric emblems of Amelia and Dobbin—"fragrant and blooming tenderly in quiet shady places"; "fluttering to Lieutenant George Osborne's heart"; "the prize I had set my life on was not worth the winning":

> The vessel is in port. He has got the prize he has been trying for all his life. The bird has come in at last. There it is with its head on his shoulder, billing and cooing close up to his heart, with soft outstretched fluttering wings. This is what he has asked for every day and hour for eighteen years. This is what he pined after. Here it

[20] Austen, *Emma,* p. 431, ch. 13.

is—the summit, the end—the last page of the third volume. Good-
bye, Colonel.—God bless you, honest William!—Farewell, dear
Amelia.—Grow green again, tender little parasite, round the rugged
old oak to which you cling! [21]

The ironic significance of this passage is a purely expressive
phenomenon; its textures are a representation of emotional realities,
rather than an illustration of rational truths. There is no logical
flaw in the premised union—Dobbin is deserving, Amelia is loving,
the marriage is appropriate. But dissonance is overt in the writer's
satirical allusion to fashionable finales ("the last page of the third
volume"), and this central discord governs a sequence of harmonic
incongruities. A rhapsody of saccharine infelicities figures the ironic
fulfillment of a fantasy: the worthless "prize" of Dobbin's chivalric
quest that began with his worship of George, "the summit" of his
pilgrimage—"the end"; Amelia's "feeble remnant" of romance that
"clings" to its victim, recalling her role, as George's bride, nesting
in "the finest tree in the whole forest" ("Grow green again, tender
little parasite")—and the subtly sacrilegious image of Amelia's
sentimental ecstasy, the "soft outstretched fluttering wings" of
dove-like devotion.

Such narrative event begins with words, and words in *Vanity
Fair* are no longer illustration. As Thackeray's writing matures, the
pastiches of *Catherine* and the *Legend* are developed into sustained dramatic metaphor: creative prose ("the expressiveness of the
word") becomes the novel's effective content. Like poetry, this
prose includes the language of emotional event; and it was the
dramatic potential of this new expressive medium that transformed
the novels of many English writers after Thackeray. The common
rhetoric of the heroine's rage in *Wuthering Heights* becomes creative
metaphor in the later novelists—in *Middlemarch*, "Titanic life gaz-
ing and struggling on walls and ceilings" of a Roman wedding
trip, an image of the heroine's "anger and repulsion"; in *The
Egoist*, a "leap for liberty"—"the intellectual halves of her clashed
like cymbals, dazing and stunning her"; and in *Tess of the D'Urbervilles*, a reflection of symbolic nature—"The evening sun was now
ugly to her, like a great inflamed wound in the sky." [22]

In *Vanity Fair*, expressive realization of emotional event is the

[21] *Works*, I, 103, ch. 12; p. 111, ch. 13; p. 658, ch. 66; p. 672, ch. 67.
[22] George Eliot, *Middlemarch*, Houghton Mifflin, Boston and New York, 1908,
I, pp. 280, 284, ch. 20; George Meredith, *The Egoist*, Charles Scribner's Sons,
New York, 1910, p. 150, ch. 13; Thomas Hardy, *Tess of the D'Urbervilles*,
Harper & Brothers, New York and London, 1928, p. 173, ch. 21.

novel's effective drama, as in the satirical mating of Dobbin and Amelia. *Vanity Fair's* dramatic "form" depends on allusive continuities—sequences of sentiment and romance—rather than on plot progressions; and these expressive sequences, their entries, their reversals, and their exits, can be graphically visualized in terms of the novel's time-span in such a way as to represent the narrative structure that readers commonly feel in the novel:

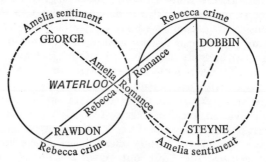

1" = 265 pp.

These patterns, evolved from expressive continuities, correspond more closely to effective form in *Vanity Fair* than analyses of literal event. The novel's opening scenes are filled with subtle discriminations in fashionable sin and sentiment—Amelia's *"Sehnsucht nach der Liebe,"* Rebecca's "Charming Alnaschar visions." At the first intimation of the heroines' future marriages, the arcs of fashionable parody are intersected by opposing tangents of chivalric satire—Amelia's "little tender heart . . . beating, and longing and trusting" to George, Becky's "barbed shaft" quivering in Rawdon's "dull hide." [23] Waterloo, the satiric paradigm of knightly combat, is *Vanity Fair's* expressive center—a sentimental-chivalric crux: the novel's opposing tangents of romance—Amelia's amorous grail-motifs, Rebecca's magic metaphors—intersect; the heroines' hostilities qualify Amelia's agony, imaged in the blood-red laceration of George's military sash; and Rebecca's victorious visit to her prostrate rival combines picaresque parody (Becky's exploits) with sentimental satire (Amelia's animosity). After the battle, chivalric oppositions are reversed. Rebecca's magical success approaches satirical apotheosis; Amelia's masochism reaches its nadir in the ironies of maternal sacrifice. As Dobbin returns, Amelia's romantic

[23] *Works,* I, 30, ch. 4; p. 18, ch. 3; p. 103, ch. 12; p. 124, ch. 14.

reprieve spans Rebecca's farcical disaster with Steyne; the swift descent of the glittering rogue is crossed by the amorous dove's ascending flight—and the final sequences are suffused with the satirical sentimentality that opened the novel.

Vanity Fair's expressive form is a vast metaphor, an extended figure filled with typifications. If the novel is named from *The Pilgrim's Progress,* its allegory begins in Bunyan's "Town . . . wherein should be sold . . . Lusts, Pleasures, and Delights of all sorts" [24]—"Yes, this is Vanity Fair," the novel's prologue announces, "eating and drinking, making love and jilting . . . not a moral place certainly; nor a merry one, though very noisy." As Thackeray's actors begin to suffer, their subjective world becomes a dramatic scene, and the novel's symbolic psychology revives the *Psycho-machia's* generic image of inner strife—a *bellum intestinum* that C. S. Lewis calls "the root of all allegory":[25] "The combat, which we describe in a sentence or two, lasted for many weeks in poor Amelia's heart . . . one by one the outworks of the little citadel were taken, in which the poor soul passionately guarded her only love and treasure." [26] But if Thackeray's initial metaphor is borrowed from Bunyan, his personifications ("behind whom all there lies a dark moral I hope"),[27] unlike the simple symbolism of *The Pilgrim's Progress,* are images of contemporary subjective complexities. Amelia is Love, but delusive love; Dobbin's Faith and Charity are colored by George's Hypocrisy; Rebecca, a moral reprobate, is also a type of Fun and Truth, the artist's persona personified. Thackeray's "Love" becomes an ambivalent quality when the novel's semi-Shakespearian commentary mocks the amorous ingenue ("Perhaps some beloved female subscriber has arrayed an ass in the splendour and glory of her imagination . . . and used him as the brilliant fairy Titania did a certain weaver at Athens.")[28] "Of course you are quite right," Thackeray remarks in a letter, "about Vanity Fair and Amelia being selfish. . . . My object is not to make a perfect character or anything like it." [29] In certain satirical perspectives the ambiguity is intensified—as when Amelia's

[24] John Bunyan, *The Pilgrim's Progress,* ed. James Blanton Wharey, The Clarendon Press, Oxford, 1928, p. 94.

[25] C. S. Lewis, *The Allegory of Love,* Oxford University Press, London, 1936, p. 68.

[26] *Works,* I, 481, ch. 50.

[27] *The Letters and Private Papers of William Makepeace Thackeray,* ed. Gordon N. Ray, Harvard University Press, Cambridge, Mass., 1964, II, 309.

[28] *Works,* I, 112, ch. 13.

[29] *Letters,* II, 309 (2 July 1847 to Mrs. Carmichael-Smyth).

pathetic poses are ironically reflected in Rebecca's insincerities. Allegory becomes a comic anti-masque when Amelia and Rebecca are beatified—when Amelia's thoughts, "as if they were angels," try "to peep into the barracks where George was"—"the gates were shut, and the sentry allowed no one to pass; so that the poor little white-robed angel could not hear the songs those young fellows were roaring over the whisky-punch." [30]—and when Rebecca, the students' "Angel Engländerin," sobs out her simulated sufferings at Baden: "it was quite evident from hearing her, that if ever there was a white-robed angel escaped from heaven to be subject to the infernal machinations and villainy of fiends here below, that spotless being—that miserable unsullied martyr, was present on the bed before Jos—on the bed, sitting on the brandy-bottle." [31]

Vanity Fair's recension of the allegory of emotional experience is the beginning of a new kind of fiction that includes such disparate exponents as Meredith, Firbank, and Virginia Woolf; it prepares a medium for such a development as *To the Lighthouse,* where drama is interior, experience subjective, fantasy fused with reality in the symbolism of World War I, as it is at Waterloo in *Vanity Fair.* But, unlike Thackeray, Virginia Woolf forces her war-metaphor to function as an objective as well as an emotional event, sacrificing the imaginative suspension of disbelief that is achieved by Thackeray's displacement of literal incident; the symbolic pattern that is sustained in *Vanity Fair* is discredited in *To the Lighthouse* by the intrusion of the realities it symbolizes.

If *Vanity Fair's* expressive method revived the techniques and typifications of Sidney, Spenser, and *The Pilgrim's Progress,* its content, like Wagner's orchestration, was a radical polyphony. "I think I see in him an intellect profounder and more unique than his contemporaries have yet recognised," Charlotte Brontë wrote. Thackeray's ability to "scrutinise and expose" seemed to her "prophet-like"—"No commentator on his writings has yet found," she insisted, "the terms which rightly characterise his talent." [32]

An aspect of this insight was Thackeray's expressive representation of psychological relativity ("after looking into a microscope how infinite littleness even is"). The glittering allusive tangents of his prose reflected a sustained ambivalent logic—a recognition of the range of possible relationships: "O philosophic reader . . . a

---

[30] *Works,* I, 111, ch. 13.
[31] *Ibid.,* p. 642, ch. 65.
[32] Charlotte Brontë, *Jane Eyre* (preface to the second edition).

distinct universe walks about under your hat and mine—all things are different to each—the woman we look at has not the same features, the dish we eat from has not the same taste to the one and the other—you and I are but a pair of infinite isolations, with some fellow-islands a little more or less near to us." [33] In *Vanity Fair,* perceptions like these fuse bits of human anomaly and fragments of shattered idealisms into eccentric images of psychological truth. "In the passage where Amelia is represented as trying to separate herself from the boy," Thackeray wrote to the critic for *Fraser's Magazine,* " 'as that poor Lady Jane Grey tried the axe that was to separate her slender life' I say that is a fine image whoever wrote it . . . it leaves you to make your own sad pictures." [34] In this sequence, the mother's suffering is mirrored in images that reflect the whole range of her sentimental neurosis —her personified denial of reality and defeat by truth, her chivalric fetishism, her amorous idolatry. The episode is conceived in several dimensions—the mother's possessiveness, her jealousy of the boy's aunt, her obsessive image of George, the child's ironic indifference—

> terror is haunting her . . . George's picture and dearest memory. . . . The child must go from her—to others—to forget her. Her heart and her treasure—her joy, hope, love, worship—her God, almost! . . . The mother had not been so well pleased, perhaps, had the rival been better looking . . . preparing him for the change . . . He was longing for it. [35]

Amelia's compulsive fantasies—"her God, almost!"—anticipating religious ironies in the novel's final love-scene, discredit the Victorian image of romantic maternity; and the allegory of Vanity Fair is largely concerned with revealing such emotional compulsions in the elements of accepted conventions. George Henry Lewes, who could accept George Eliot's ambiguities, found Thackeray's too unpleasant ("in *Vanity Fair* . . . how little there is to love") and protested the inclusion of that "detestable passage," rephrased in the prologue to *Esmond,*

> wherein [the author] adds from himself this remark:—"And who knows but Rebecca was right in her speculations—and that it was only a question of money and fortune which made the difference between her and an honest woman? . . . An alderman . . . will

[33] *Works,* II, 143, ch. 15.
[34] *Letters,* II, 424 (3 September 1848 to Robert Bell).
[35] *Works,* I, 480–85, ch. 50.

not step out of his carriage to steal . . . *but put him to starve, and see if he will not purloin a loaf.*" [Lewes' italics] Was it carelessness, or deep misanthropy, distorting an otherwise clear judgment, which allowed such a remark to fall? [36]

The passage is not personal observation; it is commentary—the rigorous recognition of the relativity of human values that typifies the novel's method. In *Vanity Fair,* the Commentator is a dimension of dissent—"I wonder is it because men are cowards in heart that they admire bravery so much"? " 'Was Rebecca guilty or not?' The Vehmgericht of the servants' hall had pronounced against her" [37]—and, instead of solving dilemmas, asks questions unanswered in the silence at the end: "Ah! *Vanitas, Vanitatum!* which of us is happy in this world? Which of us has his desire? or, having it, is satisfied?" To the *Times'* critic, Thackeray wrote "I want to leave everybody dissatisfied and unhappy at the end"—an image of reality "in that may-be cracked and warped looking glass in which I am always looking." [38]

A contingent aspect of Thackeray's insight (his power, Charlotte Brontë put it, "to penetrate the sepulchre, and reveal charnel relics") is expressed in *Vanity Fair's* mock-epic and romance evocations of primitive impulse—an imaginative projection of the hypotheses of contemporary science that became, in *The Newcomes,* a symbolism of creative method:

> Professor Owen or Professor Agassiz takes a fragment of a bone, and builds an enormous forgotten monster out of it, wallowing in primaeval quagmires, tearing down leaves and branches of plants that flourished thousands of years ago, and perhaps may be coal by this time—so the novelist puts this and that together: from the footprint finds the foot; from the foot, the brute who trod on it; from the brute, the plant he browsed on, the marsh in which he swam—and thus, in his humble way a physiologist too, depicts the habits, size, appearance of the beings whereof he has to treat;— traces this slimy reptile through the mud, and describes his habits filthy and rapacious; prods down his butterfly with a pin, and depicts his beautiful coat and embroidered waistcoat; points out the singular structure of yonder more important animal, the megatherium of his history.[39]

[36] George Henry Lewes, article on Thackeray in the *Morning Chronicle,* March 6, 1848 (quoted in the footnote for Thackeray's letter to Lewes, 6 March 1848, in *Letters,* II, 353).

[37] *Works,* I, 285, ch. 30; p. 432, ch. 44.

[38] *Letters,* II, 423–24.

[39] *Works,* VIII, 491, ch. 47.

The biological analogy is not a casual conceit; it is a newly recognized aspect of human reality that impinges on *Vanity Fair.* In Spenserian allegory, personification illustrates enduring moral fact: Una's truth, Acrasia's artifice, Guyon's discipline. The figurations of *Vanity Fair,* like Spenser's types, personify moral qualities; but Thackeray's characters express other kinds of reality as well— the survival of primitive fantasy, the persistence of the biological past. His actors are not only victims of romance delusions but types of subconscious compulsions. Primal violence is implicit at chivalric Waterloo:

> Time out of mind strength and courage have been the theme of bards and romances; and from the story of Troy down to to-day, poetry has always chosen a soldier for a hero . . . there is no end to the so-called glory and shame, and to the alternations of successful and unsuccessful murder, in which two high-spirited nations might engage. Centuries hence, we Frenchmen and Englishmen might be boasting and killing each other still.[40]

The novel's heroines exhibit atavistic symptoms: Amelia acts out archaic obsession—"powerless in the hands of her remorseless little enemy"—Rebecca reveals tribal mores—("She admired her husband, strong, brave, and victorious.")[41] Under fashionable fantasies, chivalric visions, amorous mystique, lurks the "forgotten monster" of *Vanity Fair.* The actors indulge involuntary urges— George's blood-lust, Dobbin's self-abasement, Amelia's idolatry— and *Vanity Fair's* dramatic structure is partly predicated on these emotional compulsions. Mock-epic imagery reinforces romance motif; ritual fetishes coincide (Amelia worshipping the image of George, Rebecca defacing Miss Pinkerton's doll and piercing Amelia's heart); and racial impulse becomes a sustained expressive metaphor—Sir Pitt is a "hyaena face," Rawdon a rutting bull, Dobbin a Caliban, Amelia a "bleeding heart," and Rebecca a "monster's tail," "writhing and twirling, diabolically hideous and slimy." [42]

This does not mean that *Vanity Fair* is a prototype of Conrad or Kafka; Thackeray is far more concerned with the subtleties of civilized society and the images of idealized convention. His novel is, however, a fable—and a fable with modern as well as traditional implications. Its patterns are unprecedented in English fiction;

[40] *Works,* I, 285, ch. 30; p. 311, ch. 32.
[41] *Ibid.,* p. 273, ch. 29; p. 519, ch. 53.
[42] *Ibid.,* p. 123, ch. 14; p. 246, ch. 26; p. 624, ch. 64.

but they are achieved at a sacrifice. In order to project the internal drama of *Vanity Fair*, Thackeray has excluded the dimension of objective reality and conceived his characters primarily as types. But the expressive experiment of *Vanity Fair* converges on *Henry Esmond*. The earlier novel's pilgrimage into the human heart leads on to an interpretation of "reality" in *Esmond*, where complex human actors confront both the world of subjective images and the facts of external event.

PART TWO

View Points

Frank W. Chandler: Becky as a Rogue

Rebecca Sharp, daughter of a French ballet girl and a dissipated drawing master, is perfectly passionless. She accepts the presents of the Osbornes, "after just the proper degree of hesitation," only to laugh in her sleeve at these vulgar city people. She scorns children. She abuses her own little Rawdon, and spurns her husband for his devotion to the boy. Only when she tries to captivate Sir Pitt does she hem a shirt for the child. "Whenever Mrs. Rawdon wished to be particularly humble and virtuous this little shirt used to come out of her work-box. It had got to be too small for Rawdon long before it was finished." From the moment when she begins assaults upon the susceptible Jos Sedley, through her trifling with old Sir Pitt, her capture of Rawdon, her flirtations with George Osborne and with General Tufto, and her flattery of young Sir Pitt, up to her dark intrigue with the Marquis of Steyne, and the affairs ensuing, her heart is never once engaged. She plays with these victims for personal gain. She uses and discards them. If she chance to be herself discarded, she seeks fresh conquests unperturbed. For Rawdon alone she evinces patronizing regard, until his stupidity disgusts her. When he has ridden off to Waterloo on a borrowed nag, wearing his shabbiest uniform that Becky may enjoy the larger resources in case he should fall, she re-reads George Osborne's note proposing elopement, smiles at herself in the glass, relishes her breakfast, and takes complacent account of her possessions. Later, through the years of elegant swindling in Paris and London, she merely tolerates her husband, and seeks to keep him out of the way. Once only she loses contempt for him. When in fury he strikes down Lord Steyne, we hear that "she admired her husband, strong, brave, and victorious."

Of conscience Becky knows nothing. Her breast is the scene of no conflict. From the outset she is given up to getting on in the world as she finds it. So she lavishes attentions on coarse old Sir

"*Becky as a Rogue.*" *From* The Literature of Roguery *by Frank W. Chandler (Boston: Houghton Mifflin Company, 1907), II, 463–65. Copyright 1907 by Frank W. Chandler. Reprinted by permission of the publisher.*

Pitt and on sour Miss Crawley, whose five-per-cents are coveted by
an affectionate family. When Sir Pitt goes down on his knees to
her before his wife's funeral she suffers chagrin, not at the insult,
but because, having already in secret married his son, she must
reject this offer and lose a title. She coquets with George Osborne
on his honeymoon, and gleefully wounds Amelia, her first pro-
tectress. When Rawdon grumbles that his winnings at play will
hardly discharge the inn bill, she asks, "Why need we pay it?"
She is expert in tapping admirers for presents, hinting the lack of a
watch or a jewel. She jockeys cowardly Jos out of a small fortune for
her horses when she finds him in a panic to flee from Brussels. She
lures the guileless to ruin through her husband's prowess at cards,
the dicebox, and the cue, though she is wise enough to counsel
him that "gambling, dear, is good to help your income, but not as
an income in itself." Plotting to secure something more permanent,
she spreads the report of a legacy just received, arranges their
flight from Paris, and compounds with their London creditors.
Then she sets up an establishment in Mayfair that costs next to
nothing, inasmuch as all the servants and tradesmen are owed and
forced to keep interest in her welfare, while gallant gentlemen
furnish the larder and the cellar.

She swindles the retired family butler, her landlord, pretends to
invest while she appropriates the savings of her sheep-dog companion, Miss Briggs, diverts to herself whatever gifts of money
are made to her little boy, appears on her presentation at court in
laces and brocades which she has abstracted from the wardrobes
while putting Sir Pitt's house to rights, and seriously reflects, "I
think I could be a good woman if I had five thousand a year." She
flatters Sir Pitt until he exclaims, "How that woman comprehends
me!" When the sardonic Marquis of Steyne, friend of his Glorious
Majesty, and "with all his stars, garters, collars, and cordons" suc-
cumbs to her wiles, he obliges his wife to invite Becky to Gaunt
House, sends young Rawdon to school, procures an office for old
Rawdon, and is enchanted with even her attempts to deceive him.
"What an accomplished little devil it is," he cries; "what a splendid
actress and manager! She is unsurpassable in lies."

Becky's mendacity is, indeed, so usual that the reader does not
know whether to believe her protestations of innocence at the
critical moment when Rawdon, having returned unexpectedly from
the spunging-house where she had left him to languish, finds her,
glittering with diamonds, smiling up in the face of the Marquis,
who is stooping to kiss her hand.

The misfortunes that follow during years of lonely privateering cannot awake in her a conscience, and when worn and disreputable she comes on Dobbin, Amelia, and Jos, the only piece of honesty to her credit is the impulsive disabusing of Amelia's mind, so long under the delusion that her George had been a saint. In everything else Becky cheats as always. And when Jos, after having insured his life in her behalf, suddenly dies, the solicitor of the company pronounces it a black case.

Percy Lubbock: Thackeray's Authorial Intrusion

But Thackeray—in *his* story we need him all the time and can never forget him. He it is who must assemble and arrange his large chronicle, piecing it together out of his experience. Becky's mode of life, in his story, is a matter of many details picked up on many occasions, and the power that collects them, the mind that contains them, is always and openly Thackeray's; it could not be otherwise. It is no question, for most of the time, of watching a scene at close quarters, where the simple, literal detail, such as anybody might see for himself, would be sufficient. A stretch of time is to be shown in perspective, at a distance; the story-teller must be at hand to work it into a single impression. And thus the general panorama, such as Thackeray displays, becomes the representation of the author's experience, and the author becomes a personal entity, about whom we may begin to ask questions. Thackeray *cannot* be the nameless abstraction that the dramatist (whether in the drama of the stage or in that of the novel) is naturally. I know that Thackeray, so far from trying to conceal himself, comes forward and attracts attention and nudges the reader a great deal more than he need; he likes the personal relation with the reader and insists on it. But do what he might to disguise it, so long as he is ranging over his story at a height, chronicling, summarizing, foreshortening, he *must* be present to the reader as a narrator and a showman. It is only when he descends and approaches a certain occasion and sets a scene with due circumspection—rarely and a trifle awkwardly—that he can for the time being efface the thought of his active part in the affair.

———
"Thackeray's Authorial Intrusion." From The Craft of Fiction *by Percy Lubbock (London: Jonathan Cape Limited, 1921; New York: The Viking Press, Inc., 1957), pp. 113–15. All rights reserved. Reprinted by permission of the publishers.*

So much of a novel, therefore, as is not dramatic enactment, not *scenic,* inclines always to picture, to the reflection of somebody's mind. Confronted with a scene—like Becky's great scene—we forget that other mind; but as soon as the story goes off again into narrative a question at once arises. *Who* is disposing the scattered facts, whose is this new point of view? It is the omniscient author, and the point of view is his—such would be the common answer, and it is the answer we get in Vanity Fair. By convention the author is allowed his universal knowledge of the story and the people in it. But still it is a convention, and a prudent novelist does not strain it unnecessarily. Thackeray in Vanity Fair is not at all prudent; his method, so seldom strictly dramatic, is one that of its nature is apt to force this question of the narrator's authority, and he goes out of his way to emphasize the question still further. He flourishes the fact that the point of view is his own, not to be confounded with that of anybody in the book. And so his book, as one may say, is not complete in itself, not really self-contained; it does not meet and satisfy all the issues it suggests. Over the whole of one side of it there is an inconclusive look, something that draws the eye away from the book itself, into space. It is the question of the narrator's relation to the story.

E. M. Forster: Becky as a "Round Character"

She [the Countess in Meredith's *Evan Harrington*] is a flat character. Becky is round. She, too, is on the make, but she cannot be summed up in a single phrase, and we remember her in connection with the great scenes through which she passed and as modified by those scenes—that is to say, we do not remember her so easily because she waxes and wanes and has facets like a human being. All of us, even the sophisticated, yearn for permanence, and to the unsophisticated permanence is the chief excuse for a work of art. We all want books to endure, to be refuges, and their inhabitants to be always the same, and flat characters tend to justify themselves on this account.

"Becky as a 'Round Character.'" From Aspects of the Novel *by E. M. Forster (New York: Harcourt, Brace & World, Inc.; London: Edward Arnold [Publishers] Ltd., 1927), pp. 106–7. Copyright 1927 by Harcourt, Brace & World, Inc. Reprinted by permission of the publishers.*

Edwin Muir: The Novel of Character

The novel of character is one of the most important divisions in prose fiction. Probably the purest example of it in English literature is *Vanity Fair*. *Vanity Fair* has no "hero"; no figures who exist to precipitate the action; no very salient plot; no definite action to which everything contributes; no end towards which all things move. The characters are not conceived as parts of the plot; on the contrary they exist independently, and the action is subservient to them. Whereas in the novel of action particular events have specific consequences, here the situations are typical or general, and designed primarily to tell us more about the characters, or to introduce new characters. As long as this is done anything within probability may happen. The author may invent his plot as he goes along, as we know Thackeray did. Nor need the action spring from an inner development, from a spiritual change in the characters. It need not show us any new quality in them, and at the time when it is manifested. All it need do is to bring out their various attributes, which were there at the beginning; for these characters are almost always static. They are like a familiar landscape, which now and then surprises us when a particular effect of light or shadow alters it, or we see it from a new prospect. Amelia Sedley, George Osborne, Becky Sharp, Rawdon Crawley—these do not change as Eustacia Vye and Catherine Earnshaw do; the alteration they undergo is less a temporal one than an unfolding in a continuously widening present. Their weaknesses, their vanities, their foibles, they possess from the beginning and never lose to the end; and what actually does change is not these, but our knowledge of them.

"The Novel of Character." From The Structure of the Novel *by Edwin Muir (London: Hogarth Press Ltd., 1929), pp. 23–25. Reprinted by permission of Mrs. Willa Muir and the publisher.*

Geoffrey Tillotson: "Panorama" and "Scene"

This consideration of drama, novel and history brings us to Mr Lubbock's terms, "panorama" and "scene." Both terms he illustrates

---

" 'Panorama' and 'Scene.' " From Thackeray the Novelist *by Geoffrey Tillotson (New York: Cambridge University Press, 1954), pp. 82–84. Reprinted by permission of the publisher.*

from *Vanity Fair*. It is as a scene that he takes Thackeray's presentation of the incident that marks the major crisis in Becky's fortunes. Hitherto we have had "panorama"—

> we have been listening to Thackeray, on the whole, while he talked about Becky—talked with such extraordinary brilliance that he evoked her in all her ways and made us see her with his eyes; but now it is time to see her with our own. . . .[1]

We misunderstand Thackeray's method, however, unless we see that Mr Lubbock exaggerates the extent of the shift. He errs in describing the "scene" as "strictly dramatic." That no scene in Thackeray ever is, except, of course, those few tête-à-tête conversations, which, for economy's sake and with a glance at the contemporary stage, he prints as drama. With that exception, the presenter of the scene is always seen performing the act of presenting it, treating it as if it were also panorama. To look more closely at Mr Lubbock's instance, and to begin with the setting: Rawdon, we are told,

> walked home rapidly. It was nine o'clock at night. He ran across the streets, and the great squares of Vanity Fair, and at length came up breathless opposite his own house. He started back and fell against the railings, trembling as he looked up. The drawing-room windows were blazing with light. She had said that she was in bed and ill. He stood there for some time, the light from the rooms on his pale face.[2]

So far this preliminary is panorama, with one moment's recourse by the author to omniscience: we are given the inside of Rawdon's mind in "She had said that she was in bed and ill." Apart from this one sentence—and even that evinces knowledge of an external fact, what Becky had written in her letter, not knowledge of thought—we discern Rawdon's mind only on the evidence of our eyes: which is plentiful evidence—witness "rapidly . . . across . . . at length . . . breathless . . . started . . . fell . . . trembling . . . for some time . . . pale." But even in this passage, Thackeray is more than a pair of eyes—more, however, not because he enters the minds of his personages, but because he gives us his own. If it is Rawdon who is observed to run across the streets and squares, it is "the person writing" who calls the squares "great," for "great" is ironic and Rawdon is in no mood for literary refinements. Nor in

---

[1] Percy Lubbock, *The Craft of Fiction* (edition of 1929), p. 100.
[2] *Vanity Fair*, ch. LIII.

any mood for the periphrasis, painful as it is, of "the wretched woman":

> Rawdon opened the door and went in. A little table with a dinner was laid out—and wine and plate. Steyne was hanging over the sofa on which Becky sate. The wretched woman was in a brilliant full toilette.

In the scene that follows we have aural experience added to ocular —words are spoken and we hear them. But at this point, too, we get something more. The "person writing" not only sees and hears but comments. When Rawdon has flung Lord Steyne to the ground, we are told not only what might have been seen by any sharp-eyed on-looker, that Rebecca "stood there trembling before him," but also what could only have been seen by eyes sharpened on the flint of a mind's power of insight, that "she admired her husband, strong, brave, victorious." And it is "the person writing" who adds the remote, cool, Homeric touch, a touch also of the mock-heroic such as Thackeray often added to his narrative:

> [Rawdon] tore the diamond ornament out of her breast, and flung it at Lord Steyne. It cut him on his bald forhead. Steyne wore the scar to his dying day.

And if Thackeray intended an echo of the phrase "wore the star," that is another ironic touch added from outside the scene.

Thackeray has scenes by the hundred. I do not give much weight to Mr Lubbock's remark that he jibbed at big ones. It may happen once or twice in *Vanity Fair*. But on the whole his novels are a string of scenes of all sizes. With his aspiration to hear his persons speak, how could it be otherwise? But even in a scene Thackeray is panoramic also, and he distances the picture and conversations by his own commentary on them.

Walter Allen: Thackeray's Trivial View of Life

No novelist of genius has given us an analysis of man in society based on so trivial a view of life. This is implicit in the very title *Vanity Fair*, which has a very different meaning for Thackeray from that which it had for Bunyan. For Bunyan Vanity Fair repre-

---

"Thackeray's Trivial View of Life." From The English Novel *by Walter Allen (London: J. M. Dent & Sons Ltd.; New York: E. P. Dutton & Co., Inc., 1954), pp. 200–201. Reprinted by permission of the author and publisher.*

sents the whole of society and indeed all men's activities except one. For him, it is the World itself, and therefore of the Devil. The world's activities are vanity because they lead to damnation; every moment in Bunyan immortal souls are in the balance. With Thackeray the word vanity and the whole concept of Vanity Fair have undergone a change in meaning. In effect he is taking Bunyan's Vanity Fair at the valuation not of Christian but of its most respected inhabitants. He is not approving, but neither is he disapproving—much. Vanity is no longer that which is empty and worthless, a snare and a delusion, a trip wire on the path to salvation; it is simply self-esteem, the desire to be thought well of by the world. This, for Thackeray, has become the motive of human behavior. "Wherever there was a man, he saw a snob"; and snobbery, the jockeying for social position and the pretense to a status rather higher than the person's true one he saw as the main driving force of man in society.

Joseph E. Baker: Thackeray and St. Augustine

The *City of God* and *Vanity Fair* may be read as the philosophical generalization and the concrete illustration of the vanity of worldly desires. For Thackeray was a poet by Sidney's definition, "fayning notable images of virtues and vices, or what else, with that delightful teaching which must be the right describing note to know a Poet by . . . But the poet is the foode for the tenderest stomacks, the Poet is indeed the right Popular Philosopher."

I do not mean to say that Thackeray and St. Augustine were in complete agreement, but they were closer together than is popularly supposed. St. Augustine makes clear that the world is not given over to wickedness, for there is righteousness even in the world. His "earthly city" is not the whole life of society, but rather an abstraction; as Thackeray's fair of vanities is a very real fiction. Both authors present a picture of life as it *would be* without the spiritual. To take this for "man as he is" constitutes a profound misunderstanding. Critics have often discussed Thackeray as if he meant to give us in *Vanity Fair* a complete record of human life; for the very breadth and scope of the novel tempt the reader

"Thackeray and St. Augustine." From "Vanity Fair *and the Celestial City" by Joseph E. Baker in* Nineteenth Century Fiction, X *(1955), 93–94. Copyright © 1955 by The Regents of the University of California. Reprinted by permission of The Regents and the author.*

to forget that Thackeray's own view of life has even greater breadth and scope than this picture. The world of the novel has no art, no science, no poetry, no statesmanship, no philosophy, no scholarship. Thackeray quite consciously made a selection of materials for his puppet show, and at one point mentions the limits he has set for himself. Speaking of Amelia—

> Love had been her faith hitherto, and the sad, bleeding, disappointed heart began to feel the want of another consoler. Have we a right to repeat or to overhear her prayers? These, brother, are secrets, and out of the domain of Vanity Fair, in which our story lies.[1]

Perhaps he had to treat them as "secrets" because he did not find his style adequate to render celestial realities without falling into what he felt to be "cant phrases." Similarly, I think we can say that Thackeray was a great thinker but never wrote philosophy. But English philosophy itself, since the seventeenth century, had not gone beyond a study of "the natural man," while those who were the conscious heirs and successors of Bunyan were hopelessly entangled in the cant phrase. That is why, in appreciating Thackeray's mentality, we must turn not to his immediate predecessors in English prose but to St. Augustine.

E. M. W. Tillyard: Vanity Fair: A Picaresque Romance

Among Thackeray's novels *Vanity Fair* has the largest scope, doing greatest justice to its author's capacities; it has thence the best initial chance of touching the epic.

Amplitude of a kind it has. The characters have all the room they want to move about in; and Thackeray insists on working out their destinies without stint or hurry. He can bore us with this insistence, and yet we admire and approve his thoroughness. Thus, when Becky has suffered her great fall and goes into exile on the Continent, Thackeray refuses to allow the waning of interest, in-

---

"Vanity Fair: *A Picaresque Romance.*" *From* The Epic Strain in the English Novel *by E. M. W. Tillyard (London: Chatto & Windus Ltd.; New York: Oxford University Press, 1958), pp. 117–19. Copyright © 1958 by E. M. W. Tillyard. Reprint d by permission of Stephen Tillyard and the publishers.*

[1] Chap. XXVI.

evitable after this catastrophe, to panic him, to force him into
the least hurry. He had centred interest in Becky's gamble and
Rawdon's shifting part in it and had made it impossible to kindle
the book into its former intensity, once the issue of that gamble was
declared. Nevertheless, he goes on manfully working up and out
the things to which he has been committed. We know that Dobbin
will get his Amelia, and with one part of ourselves we deplore the
drawing out of the process. With another part of ourselves we
admire Thackeray's insistence on allowing plenty of room. Pain-
fully he constructs a new setting, the petty capital town of Pumpernickel, in which to transact the things he is pledged to. Neither
setting nor transactions can stir us like their predecessors; yet they
make their impression. Amelia and Dobbin develop unguessed in-
gredients of their characters and give the lie to those readers who
have called them static. Amelia unexpectedly tyrannises over
Dobbin; and Dobbin as unexpectedly revolts. It is this revolt which,
at long last, makes a new climax: one for which we are grateful
and which leaves its substantial mark on our minds. And, finally, the
very delay until the revelation of George Osborne's long-preserved
love-letter to Becky in Brussels urging elopement brings the plot to
rest gives the last pages a special zest. A moderate boredom, we
agree, has not been too heavy a price to pay for the admirably
ample space Thackeray has allowed for his conclusion.

But amplitude of method need not imply amplitude of the
things to which the method is applied. There is amplitude in the
way Jonson works out *Volpone;* but its substance cannot claim that
quality. It would be wrong to call the world of *Vanity Fair* narrow,
for the largeness of some of the characters precludes any such
thought. But Thackeray does not animate many strata of society—
fewer than Fielding does in *Tom Jones*—indeed he is rather
puzzled by his age than familiar with it in depth. Thus limited, he
cannot voice its "accepted unconscious metaphysic."

Nor does Thackeray achieve an epic through the inclusiveness
and symbolic effect of his characters. It would be vain to argue that
Becky and Amelia cover through their contrasted natures and
careers as great an area of the human mind as Arnold Bennett
meant Constance and Sophia Baines to cover in the *Old Wives'
Tale*. Each in her way is too extreme; and anyhow Becky dwarfs
her opposite. If Becky is truly paired with anyone, it is with her
own husband, Rawdon Crawley. It is this pairing and the su-
premacy of the pair that should inform us that the literary kind
to which *Vanity Fair* most nearly belongs is not the epic but the

picaresque romance. *Vanity Fair,* even if much nobler, is the logical heir of *Barry Lyndon,* which it succeeded in time. Becky and Rawdon are both adventurers and for a while they join in preying on society. They are also among the select repertory of the major characters in world fiction. In every other way they differ. And this diversity-in-likeness gives the novel its own richness as well as its master motive. The picaresque story . . . is a genuine literary kind because it is based on a permanent proclivity of human nature; the proclivity to sympathise with anti-social behaviour while knowing that it cannot go on for ever. Falstaff and his rejection are its most famous expression in English. The careers of Rawdon and Becky furnish a superb example of it. We want Becky to win her gambles, until Rawdon develops a human affection and the beginning of a moral sense. Then we waver, and Rawdon becomes the successful agent of a transfer of feelings which many people still believe Shakespeare to have failed at when he made Falstaff lose his gamble.

There is also a good deal of support for the central item, the adventures of Becky and Rawdon. There are other adventurers besides themselves. Old Osborne is the successful adventurer in business; the self-made man. Joe Sedley, timid as he is, adventures for money in India. Young Osborne is the *parvenu* among the aristocrats who fill the commissions in the British Army. Most of the characters are or have been on the make and they unite to give the novel its special character. The disinterestedness of Amelia and Dobbin is a smaller affair and serves as a foil rather than forms the main substance. There can be no question of *Vanity Fair's* being an epic; it remains the superlative picaresque romance.

Table of Serial Publication of Vanity Fair

	Date	Chapters	Number
1847	Jan.	I–IV	1
	Feb.	V–VII	2
	Mar.	VIII–XI	3
	Apr.	XII–XIV	4
	May	XV–XVIII	5
	June	XIX–XXII	6
	July	XXIII–XXV	7
	August	XXVI–XXIX	8
	Sept.	XXX–XXXII	9
	Oct.	XXXIII–XXXV	10
	Nov.	XXXVI–XXXVIII	11
	Dec.	XXXIX–XLII	12
1848	Jan.	XLIII–XLVI	13
	Feb.	XLVII–L	14
	Mar.	LI–LIII	15
	Apr.	LIV–LVI	16
	May	LVII–LX	17
	June	LXI–LXIII	18
	July	LXIV–LXVII	19–20

Chronology of Important Dates

	Thackeray	The Age
1811	Thackeray born.	
1815		The Battle of Waterloo.
1832		Passage of the First Reform Bill.
1833	Loss of fortune.	Publication of Carlyle's *Sartor Resartus* (until 1834). The abolition of slavery in the British Empire.
1836	Marries Isabella Shawe.	Publication of Dickens' *The Pickwick Papers* (until 1837).
1837		Victoria becomes Queen.
1840	Isabella Thackeray's mental illness becomes severe.	
1842	Begins to write for *Punch*.	The Chartist Riots.
1845		The conversion of J. H. Newman to Roman Catholicism.
1847	Completion of *The Book of Snobs* (begun in 1846). Publication of *Vanity Fair* (until 1848).	Publication of Emily Brontë's *Wuthering Heights* and Charlotte Brontë's *Jane Eyre.*
1850	Completion of *Pendennis* (begun in 1848).	Posthumous publication of Wordsworth's *The Prelude.* Publication of Tennyson's *In Memoriam: A. H. H.*

1852	*Esmond*. Begins first lecture tour of the U.S.: *The English Humourists of the 18th Century*.	Death of Wellington. Opening of the New Houses of Parliament. Publication of Dickens' *Bleak House* (until 1853).
1855	Completion of *The Newcomes* (begun in 1853). Begins second lecture tour of the U.S.: *The Four Georges*.	The Crimean War (1854–56). Publication of Browning's *Men and Women*.
1859	Completion of *The Virginians* (begun in 1858). Becomes editor of the *Cornhill Magazine* (until 1862). First of *The Roundabout Papers*.	Publication of Darwin's *The Origin of Species*, Mill's *On Liberty*, Eliot's *Adam Bede*, Meredith's *The Ordeal of Richard Feverel*, FitzGerald's *Rubaiyat of Omar Khayyam*.
1863	*Philip*. Thackeray dies.	

Notes on the Editor and Contributors

M. G. SUNDELL, Associate Professor of English at Case Western Reserve University, has published articles on various nineteenth-century writers.

WALTER ALLEN is an eminent novelist as well as a literary critic. His works include a biography of George Eliot and a study of the modern novel.

JOSEPH E. BAKER, Professor of English and Chairman of the Interdepartment of European Literature and Thought at the University of Iowa, is the author of *The Novel and the Oxford Movement.*

FRANK W. CHANDLER was Professor of English at the Polytechnic Institute of Brooklyn and Lecturer in Comparative Literature at Columbia University.

G. ARMOUR CRAIG, Professor of English at Amherst College, is author of several critical essays on the novel.

A. E. DYSON, co-editor of *Critical Quarterly,* has published (with C. B. Cox) *Modern Poetry: Studies in Practical Criticism* as well as many articles on nineteenth-century literature.

E. M. FORSTER is the distinguished novelist best known for *A Passage to India.*

ARNOLD KETTLE, Senior Lecturer in English Literature at the University of Leeds, is the author of *Karl Marx: Founder of Modern Communism* and editor of *Shakespeare in a Changing World.*

JOHN LOOFBOUROW is Associate Professor of English at Boston College.

PERCY LUBBOCK, best known for *The Craft of Fiction,* also wrote a study of Edith Wharton and edited the letters of Henry James.

EDWIN MUIR was an eminent Scottish poet, novelist, and critic.

GEOFFREY TILLOTSON, Professor of English at Birkbeck College, the University of London, is a noted editor and critic. Among his works are *The Poetry of Pope* and (with Mrs. Tillotson) *Mid-Victorian Studies.*

KATHLEEN TILLOTSON is Professor of English at Bedford College, the University of London. She is the author (with the late John Butt) of *Dickens at Work* and editor of the authoritative edition of *Oliver Twist*.

E. M. W. TILLYARD was Master of Jesus College, Cambridge University, and University Lecturer in English. Among his many scholarly works are *The Elizabethan World Picture, The Miltonic Setting,* and *The English Epic and Its Background.*

DOROTHY VAN GHENT was most recently Professor of English at the State University of New York at Buffalo.

Selected Bibliography

Betsky, Seymour, "Society in Thackeray and Trollope," in *From Dickens to Hardy*, ed. Boris Ford. Baltimore, 1958. Becky as an agent for satirizing the malevolent effects of economic expansion.

Cecil, Lord David, "William Makepeace Thackeray," in *Early Victorian Novelists*. London, 1934. Reprinted as *Victorian Novelists*. Chicago, 1958. Thackeray's power to generalize depends on his mastery of parallel structure and tone.

Dodds, John W., *Thackeray: A Critical Portrait*. London, 1941. A dependable survey of the growth of Thackeray's mind. Chapter Six centers on *Vanity Fair*.

Lester, John A., Jr., "Thackeray's Narrative Technique," *PMLA*, LXIX (1954), 392–409. Thackeray's handling of chronological sequence and narrative point of view.

Ray, Gordon N., ed., *The Letters and Private Papers of William Makepeace Thackeray*. 4 vols. Cambridge, Mass., 1945–46. The starting place for any biographical study of Thackeray.

————, *Thackeray*. 2 vols. New York, 1955–58. The authoritative biography. Chapter Fourteen of the first volume is an excellent study of *Vanity Fair*.

Stevenson, Lionel, *The Showman of Vanity Fair*. New York, 1947. The best shorter biography. Chapter Ten centers on *Vanity Fair*.

Stewart, David H., "*Vanity Fair*: Life in the Void," *College English*, XXV (1963), 209–14. *Vanity Fair* as a portrait of a valueless, absurd world.

Taube, Myron, "Contrast as a Principle of Structure in *Vanity Fair*," *Nineteenth-Century Fiction*, XVIII (1963), 119–35. The structure of the work as a whole and of individual installments depends on the musical techniques of counterpoint and variation.

Wilkinson, Ann Y., "The Tomeavesian Way of Knowing the World: Technique and Meaning in *Vanity Fair*," *ELH*, XXXII (1965), 370–87. The novel as dramatic monologue.